A WALK AROUND
THE NEW FOREST

A WALK AROUND THE NEW FOREST

THIRTY-FIVE CIRCULAR WALKS

NORMAN HENDERSON

'The time will someday arrive when, as England becomes more and more over-
crowded – as each heath and common is swallowed up – the New Forest will
be as much of a necessity to the country as the parks are now to London. We
talk of the duty of reclaiming waste lands, and making corn spring up where
none before grew. But it is often as much a duty to leave them alone. Land has
higher and nobler offices to perform than to support houses or to grow corn –
to nourish not so much the body as the mind of man, to gladden the eye with
its loveliness, and to brace his soul with that strength which is alone to be
gained in the solitude of the moors and the woods.'

John R. Wise (1831–90)
The New Forest: Its History and Scenery

FRANCES LINCOLN LIMITED
PUBLISHERS

Frances Lincoln Ltd
4 Torriano Mews
Torriano Avenue
London NW5 2RZ
www.franceslincoln.com

A Walk Around the New Forest
Copyright © Frances Lincoln Ltd 2007.
Text and photographs copyright
© Norman Henderson 2007.
Maps created using data from
Ordnance Survey maps.

First Frances Lincoln edition 2007.

A catalogue record for this book is
available from the British Library.

Printed and bound in China by
Leo Paper Products Ltd.

ISBN 13: 978-0-7112-2709-5

9 8 7 6 5 4 3 2 1

CONTENTS

INTRODUCTION

Some walkers enjoy having an objective and follow some of the long-distance paths now available. The guide books for these are generally excellent, but normally they only describe the path in one direction – there's only one route after all – as though people were going to follow them on a walking holiday; however, most people do them bit by bit at weekends and, failing an arrangement with two cars or something similar, have to return the way they came. For the majority who prefer circular walks, this book provides a real long-distance journey, but one which is split into short sections, with an alternative route of return for each. The result is a series of circular walks each of which connects with the next, and which together form a complete circuit of the New Forest. The walks average about 5 miles each, so stronger walkers can combine two or three of them in a day. For those who do want a walking holiday, two itineraries are suggested – one of about 70 miles which combines the outward legs of the walks, and a second using the return legs, which add up to around 80 miles (see 'A Week's Walking', page 211).

The New Forest is an area of over 140 square miles, in much of which one is free to roam at will. Most large areas of land in England with this freedom are high moorland which is of little agricultural value except for the grazing of sheep, and the excitement is to be found in the middle of the designated area – in most of the other National Parks for example. The reasons for the openness of the New Forest, however are more political than topographical, and the beauties of its landscape persist to the very edge; the moment you step over the cattle grid, you are in a typical New Forest environment. Thus a walk around the boundary offers a real experience of what the New Forest has to offer. The typical pattern of these walks is of an outward leg with farmland to the right and open heathland or woodland to the left, and a return leg which loops back within the Forest across open heathland or through woodland; occasionally, for variety, the return leg uses field paths outside the Forest.

Ditchend Brook

INTRODUCTION

The Perambulation

Travelling round the boundary is not a new idea. In the days before detailed maps, the only way to define the limits of the Forest, and therefore the area to which the Forest Law applied, was to walk round it and identify the features which delineated it. This activity was known as a 'perambulation', and the name is still used today. The earliest surviving record dates from the early thirteenth century, although the practice is thought to date from Saxon times. The perambulation remained substantially unchanged from the late thirteenth century until the adjacent commons were brought within it in 1964. The National Park, designated in 2005, covers a slightly larger area, but it is the previous boundary which provides your route, so you will be following a historic precedent. I hope you enjoy doing so as much as I did in exploring the walks.

Footwear

In the New Forest, there are very few places which are more than a mile from the nearest road, and the climate is benign, so with one exception no special clothing or equipment is necessary. The exception is footwear. The New Forest can be very wet and muddy underfoot – especially in wet weather of course, and always in winter. Therefore waterproof footwear is essential. Walking boots are recommended; they don't need to be of the expensive, trekking-in-Nepal variety – cheap ones will do as long as they are waterproof or can be made so with one of the proprietary preparations available in outdoor shops. The walks have been explored in most conditions, and nothing has been encountered which walking boots couldn't cope with, although in winter it has often been a close run thing.

Distances

Two figures are given for each walk. First, the total length of the circular walk then (in brackets) the length of the outward leg alone for the benefit of walkers who want to do the walks one way only. For the shorter walks, distances are also given for combining them with adjacent ones.

All distances are approximate, and are given in yards and miles. For those who can only think in metric units, yards are near enough the same as metres for walkers' purposes; to convert miles to kilometres, multiply by 3/2 or 5/3 or 8/5, whichever gives the easiest sum. There are a few heights, given in feet – divide by 3 to get metres; to be more precise, knock off another 10 per cent.

The intermediate distances in the directions show how far it is since the preceding distance was given, not just from the last instruction.

Parking

Each walk starts at somewhere to park. Most walks use designated car parks, but a few start at commonly used places on the roadside verge. Directions are given on how to get there, with approximate distances; a road atlas would be a useful supplement. Occasionally the directions take a roundabout route in order to avoid driving along a road you will later walk along. The precise spot is pinpointed by the OS map reference (if you're not familiar with the system, you'll find an explanation on all OS maps). The further end of most of the walks is at the parking place for the next one, so you can check it out in advance. The abbreviation 's.p.' means 'signposted'.

Be warned that Lyndhurst suffers from dreadful traffic jams on summer weekends and is best avoided; particularly, don't approach it from Junction 1 of the M27 at Cadnam. Instead, leave the M27 at Junction 2, take the A326 southwards, then follow signs to Lyndhurst via the A35. On the way home, make a detour by way of Picket Post or Beaulieu.

Directions

The directions were checked shortly before going to press, but please don't take any individual instruction as gospel – things do change, for example fences are put up or taken down, the growth or clearance of gorse is a particular problem, and gates are sometimes locked when forestry operations are in progress.

For those who want to do more than one walk at a time, directions are given for continuing to the next, and returning to the previous one; this text is highlighted in italic script (for example 'To continue to **Walk 31** turn right along the river bank').

INTRODUCTION

Note that a few of the walks don't quite join up with the adjacent ones and walkers who punctiliously want to be sure their circuit of the Forest is complete every step of the way should follow the instructions for joining the next walk until the connection is made; the longest of these detours takes about 10 minutes.

Pubs

The history of ownership and land use of the New Forest has resulted in many small settlements growing up at the edge, just outside the boundary, which means that many of the walks pass a pub at some point. They are mentioned in the text, and my apologies are offered to any landlord whose premises I may have missed. Be aware however that many of them have not as yet adopted the practice of all-day opening.

The Red Shoot Inn at Linwood

Near by

No program of walks can cover everything worth seeing in and around an area as large as the New Forest, so for each walk a short supplementary expedition is suggested under the heading of 'Near by', to be done by taking a roundabout route on the way home. For example, after Walk 1 you might like to go for a stroll along the foreshore at Lepe, which is just three miles away. Paying attractions are not included because you would probably want to devote more time to them than you have available after your walk.

Maps

I hope that the sketch maps and written directions will be sufficient for following the walks, but they will certainly offer no help if you miss your way and wander off the route. Therefore it would be better to regard them as a supplement to a good map such as the Ordnance Survey Explorer Map OL22, which covers the New

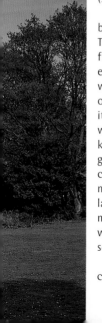

Forest and surrounding area at a scale of 1:25,000 (2½ inches to the mile).

If you're not used to walking with maps, you'll be surprised how easy it is to get completely lost. The trick is to keep the map in hand and consult it frequently. If at any time you can't pinpoint your exact position, stop, and don't move until you've worked out precisely where you are. Then work out what you should come to next, and how long it will take to reach it (get to know your own walking speed by timing yourself a few times over known distances). The most common mistake is to go blindly on regardless, saying 'we're bound to come to it soon' when in fact you have already missed your way. If you haven't come to your landmark in five or ten minutes over your estimated time, stop and repeat the process. To start with, it all seems like dreadfully hard work, but it soon becomes an easy habit.

Though not essential, a compass is handy to confirm you're still going in the right direction.

11

INTRODUCTION

The maps are not strictly to scale, priority being given to showing necessary detail. The symbols used are as follows:

════	Surfaced road
═ ═-═-═	Track or unsurfaced road
─ ─ ─ ─-	Path
─+─+─	Railway line
─ (─(─	Route of former railway
────	Fence or hedge (where relevant)
─o─	Boundary (usually followed by a fence)
∼∼∼	Stream
Ⓟ	Car park
P̲	Other parking
──→	Direction of walk
⟹	Direction to adjacent walk
A	Cross-reference to text
↑	North

Note that the definition of a 'track' is rather arbitrary; the forest roads are shown as tracks, whereas the 'rides' (grassy avenues through the trees) are usually shown as paths. No distinction is made between paths and bridleways.

Local Information and Accommodation

There are Visitor Information Centres at Lyndhurst (023 8028 2269), Lymington (01590 689000), Ringwood (01425 470896), and Fordingbridge (01425 654560).

Local information and an accommodation guide are available from The New Forest District Council (022380 285464 or www.thenewforest.co.uk), and information about the Forestry Commission caravan and camping sites is provided by Forest Holidays (0131 314 6505 or www.forestholidays.co.uk). Other useful accommodation lists can be found on the internet.

Public Transport

Routes pass within a mile or so of many of the walks, providing you accept that you may not join a walk at the start of its circuit. More will be accessible if you join two walks together, timetables permitting, or book an occasional night in a B&B.

The railway stations at Ashurst, Sway, and Brockenhurst can be used for Walks 7, 8, 27, 28, 29 and 31.

Useful bus routes are: Southampton to Fawley, Southampton to Salisbury, Southampton to Bournemouth, Salisbury to Bournemouth and Lymington to Hythe. Walks 14, 15, 16 and 19 are a bit further away from the main routes.

For more energetic walkers, the Southampton to Hythe ferry (which carries cycles free) lands about 2 miles away from Walks 3, 4 and 5, and Lymington Pier station is about 2 miles away from Walks 32, 33 and 34.

Travel information can be found at:

Traveline 0870 608 2 608 — www.traveline.org.uk
National Rail Enquiries 08457 484950 — www.nationalrail.co.uk
Hampshire County Council www3.hants.gov.uk/passengertransport
or see:
South West Trains 0845 6000 650 — www.swtrains.co.uk
Virgin Trains 08457 222333 — www.virgintrains.co.uk
Solent Blue Line 023 8061 8233 — www.solentblueline.com
Wilts and Dorset Bus Co. 01202 673555 — www.wdbus.co.uk
Hythe Ferry 02380 840722 — www.hytheferry.co.uk

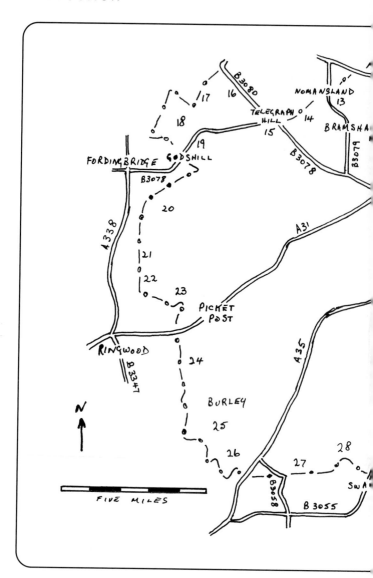

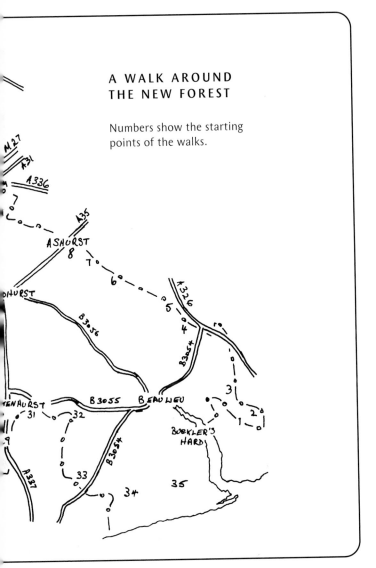

A WALK AROUND THE NEW FOREST

Numbers show the starting points of the walks.

INTRODUCTION

Thanks

Most of my knowledge of the New Forest was gleaned from books in the excellent 'Local Interest' section of Southampton City Library. I am grateful to the authors and hope I have represented their work accurately.

The New Forest is a special place, and remains so only because of the efforts of many people and organisations to whom we all owe a debt of gratitude – particularly to the Forestry Commission in carrying out its duty of care, and especially to the Commoners; without the dedicated pursuit of their customs, not always in the easiest of circumstances, the Forest would not have survived in its present form.

Take Care

As far as I am aware all the walks are on public rights of way or access land, and the parking places are appropriate and available for public use; however I cannot guarantee this, and readers should satisfy themselves as to these matters. I have come to no harm in my explorations, but walkers must of course take responsibility for their own safety, for example on roads or with animals.

Of course I don't need to remind you to follow the Country Code, but look out for notices advising of local circumstances – for example keeping to the paths in springtime so as not to disturb ground-nesting birds.

One More Thing

Don't feed or pet the ponies – you will occasionally see notices explaining why not. They are docile creatures more interested in grass than in you, but they can sometimes be aggressive at car parks where people have fed them titbits – and be careful not to get yourself between a mare and her foal.

The Knightwood Oak

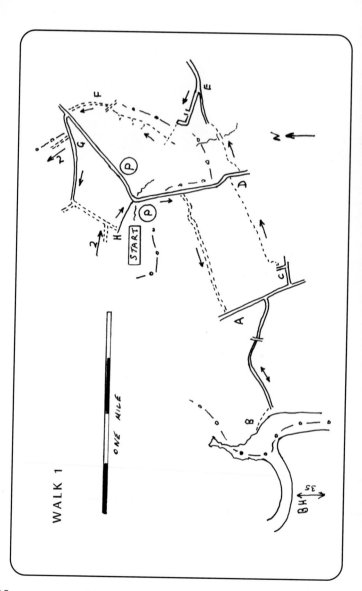

WALK 1

ONE MILE

WALK 1: GILBURY
TO BLACKWELL COMMON

DISTANCE 5½ miles (4½ miles)

PARKING Dark Water car park (SU 433014)

From the A326 (Totton to Fawley): pass through Holbury towards
Fawley and take the right fork at the roundabout (7¾ miles from
the A35, s.p. Blackfield); go through the traffic lights (⅓ mile) then
proceed from * below.

From the west: go through Beaulieu on the B3054 (s.p. Hythe); turn
right by The Royal Oak (1 mile, s.p. Holbury – don't turn right
again to Exbury). Turn right at the traffic lights (2½ miles), then
* turn right at the crossroads (⅓ mile, opposite The Hampshire
Yeoman) into Exbury Road. Pass Blackwell Common car park
(⅔ mile). Dark Water car park is on the right as the road climbs out
of the dip (¼ mile).

There are a few places where the New Forest boundary cannot be
followed on the ground because of private land or patches of bog,
but the only point where it cannot even be followed theoretically
(unless you know somebody with a boat) is where it crosses the
Beaulieu River; this is the obvious place to start your circumper-
ambulation. From the shore at Gilbury Hard (B) there is a good view
of the finishing point, Bucklers Hard (BH), only half a mile away as
the crow flies but nearly 80 miles on foot for the Forest circum-
perambulator. This point is only accessible by one route, so despite
my promise of circular walks, this one involves some retracing of
steps.

Exbury Gardens (A) were created in the years between the two
world wars by Lionel de Rothschild, who bought the estate in 1919;
they cover 200 acres, are open for most of the year and are best
known for the spectacular display of rhododendrons and azaleas in
spring. The gardens are bisected by Gilbury Lane, which runs down
to the Beaulieu River (B). The banks either side of the road are
covered in rhododendrons, and there is the surprise of the grace-

The Beaulieu River at Gilbury Hard

ful Exbury Bridge, which crosses the quiet lane to join the two parts of the gardens.

The Manor of Exbury was first recorded in the thirteenth century, stretching from the Beaulieu River to Dark Water. The village (C) was once known as Gilbury, the name 'Exbury' being used for what is now Lower Exbury. You will pass the church, dating from 1907, the entrance to the Exbury estate offices with its tall brick tower, the old post office, perhaps once a substantial business but now a private dwelling, and a pair of antique petrol pumps.

Lawn Cemetery (F) adjoins the site on which Blackfield Baptist Church stood from 1830 to 1939 when it was replaced by a chapel in the village; the cemetery is now in the care of the New Forest District Council. The oldest graves are at the far end as you walk, and down to the right. They include one which mourns the loss of four young children from the same family, all of whom died within a few weeks of each other; how lucky we are to have the benefits of modern medicine.

As you walk on the heath, you will see hills about 10 miles away to the south. They are on the Isle of Wight, rising to around 700 feet, and are an almost constant feature of views from the Forest.

Directions

From the car park turn right on the road; turn right on the track (300 yds – look back for the footpath sign; this track is used as the exit road from the overflow car park of Exbury Gardens and can be busy in spring); keep right around the farm house. Turn left on the road by the entrance to Exbury Gardens (A, ²/₃ mile, Summer Lane).

Take the first right (300 yds, Gilbury Lane). At the end (½ mile) turn right on the path to the shore (B, 200 yds). This is where the journey starts; take a good look across to Bucklers Hard to keep it in mind during the walk to come.

Return to Summer Lane and turn right. Turn left in Exbury village (200 yds) then first left by the post box (C, 200 yds, s.p. Footpath). Follow the track to the right (100 yds), turn left along the edge of the field, then right on the footpath along the edge of the wood to Exbury Road (D, ½ mile). Turn right.

Turn left on the footpath just after Sturt Cottages (100 yds). Shortly after crossing Dark Water it becomes a road (⅓ mile); turn sharp left at the junction (E, 300 yds). Follow this road to the end (¼ mile), turn left through the gate, climb the rising ground beyond and turn right (200 yds) on the path along the edge of the heath.

At the back gate of the cemetery (F, ⅓ mile) turn left, cross Exbury Road (⅓ mile) into King's Copse Road and follow it round to the left.

For **Walk 2**, turn right between houses called 'Sugar Loaf' and 'Red Roofs' (G, 200 yds). Otherwise go on to the end of the road (⅓ mile) and bear left on the track ahead to its end by a smallholding (H, ¼ mile, **Walk 2** rejoins here). Turn left along the hedge to the road at Gatewood Bridge (300 yds), and turn right to the car park (200 yds).

Near by

At **Lepe Country Park** (3 miles) you can stroll along the foreshore or the low cliffs and enjoy broad views across the Solent to the Isle of Wight, about 2 miles away – Lepe is a short way west of Cowes.

• Turn right out of Dark Water car park then take the first left (1 mile). There is a pay-and-display car park part way along the shore road and larger one further on (2 miles, SZ 455985) with a restaurant, shop, ice cream kiosk and information centre.

WALK 2: BLACKWELL COMMON TO HOLBURY

DISTANCE 5 miles (2 miles)

PARKING Blackwell Common car park (SU 436016)

From the A326 (Totton to Fawley): pass through Holbury towards Fawley and take the right fork at the roundabout (7¾ miles from the A35, s.p. Blackfield); go through the traffic lights (⅓ mile) then proceed from * below.

From the west: go through Beaulieu on the B3054 (s.p. Hythe); turn right by The Royal Oak (1 mile, s.p. Holbury – don't turn right again to Exbury). Turn right at the traffic lights (2½ miles), then * turn right at the crossroads (⅓ mile, opposite The Hampshire Yeoman) into Exbury Road. The car park is on the left (⅔ mile).

A short walk across the common brings you to a leafy lane with pastures either side and oaks overhead, which leads to a woodland stretch by the western fringes of Holbury and to Holbury Manor Park (C). The manor of Holbury was first recorded in 1312 and was granted to Beaulieu Abbey. Holbury Mill fell out of use after the Dissolution; it gave its name to The Old Mill Inn (D). The reedy millpond, much silted up, is to the right where Walk 3 rejoins the route.

The area covered in the first three walks is drained by Dark Water, which is 5 miles long and flows into the Solent at Lepe. The loop round the Country Heritage Site (D to E) passes beside its gathering grounds – this swamp is the reason for the detours of Walk 3. After a mile across the heath (E to G) the walk goes through King's Copse Inclosure (G to H), following the Dark Water valley; the forest road is lined for much of the way by broad-leaved trees, including oak, birch and sweet chestnut.

The stacks of the Esso Fawley Refinery on the skyline are surprisingly less obtrusive than they might be, the lower parts being

Lawn Cemetery

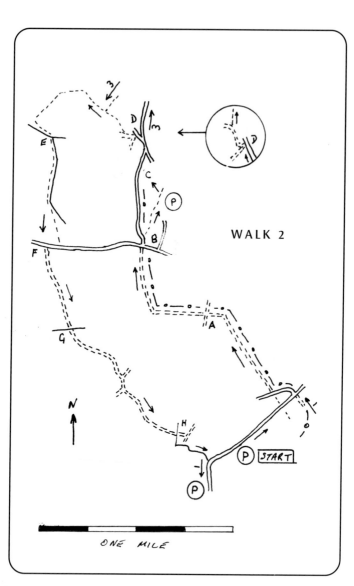

WALK 2

N

ONE MILE

24

mostly screened by trees round the edge of the site; the locations of Fawley and Dibden Inclosures (Walks 3 and 4) were chosen to provide further visual screening of the industrial area. The refinery was built on an older site in the 1950s, and benefits from Southampton Water being deep enough here to berth large tankers. The most obvious sign of refinery activity is the flare stack, which is not burning off waste products as is often supposed – it is a safety feature, and the flame is a pilot light; in an emergency, inflammable substances can be diverted up the flare stack and burned off safely, reducing the risk of fire or explosion. The tallest chimney of all, a mile further to the south-east, is at Fawley Power Station, which burns oil received direct from the refinery. If the traffic on the A326 was less than you expected, it's because most of the refinery output is sent by pipeline and by sea. Some also goes by rail along the Fawley branch, which joins the main line at Totton; it opened in 1925 and passenger services ended in 1966, but it is still open for freight and also gives access to the military port at Marchwood.

The Old Mill Inn is at the far end of the walk (D), and The Bridge Tavern is near the route (between B and F).

Directions

Turn right along the road then left on a well worn path (⅓ mile) and cross Kings Copse Road (100 yds) on to the track between 'Red Roofs' and 'Sugar Loaf'. *Walk 1 joins here.* After a left-hand bend and a crossing by a cattle grid (A, ½ mile), go straight on through a gate. Turn right with the lane at the entrance to the Green Rollestone Estate and cross Rollestone Road into Park Lane (B, ½ mile).

Immediately bear right into the wood (20 yds) and follow the path, which keeps houses in sight to the right (if you come to the road just turn left along it). At Holbury Manor Park (¼ mile) the car park for Walk 3 is near by on the right. Bear left across the grass to a gap in the trees leading to the pond (C, 200 yds). Turn left to the gate and turn right in Park Lane (50 yds).

Turn left at the junction (200 yds). *For **Walk 3** go straight on.* Otherwise turn left again (50 yds) towards The Old Mill Inn. Turn

Green Lane

left at the bottom (D, 200 yds) and cross the stile beside the gate in the right fork. Follow the track a short way then turn right on a waymarked path. Stay down in the valley (***Walk 3 rejoins here***) until the path climbs to an area of thin pasture and becomes indistinct (²/₃ mile). Go straight ahead to the fence (200 yds) and turn left along it. Cross a stile on the right (E, 200 yds) and continue by the fence on the left; when it bears away left, go straight on to the road (F, ½ mile).

Cross into the track with a cycleway sign which leads to the gate into King's Copse Inclosure (G, ½ mile); follow it through the inclosure (at the junction it bears right then left) to

Blackwell Common (H, ¾ mile). Turn right and follow the track then the hedge to the road (¼ mile). *To return to Walk 1 turn right.* Otherwise turn left to the car park (¼ mile).

Near by
Calshot Spit (3½ miles) at the mouth of Southampton Water is a half-mile shingle spit which offers views of the Solent and Southampton Water and the associated boating and shipping. After a long row of colourful beach huts is an area of various activity centres, including a large sports hall occupying a former flying boat hanger. At the end is Calshot Castle, built by Henry VIII as part of his coastal defences, using stone from Beaulieu Abbey.

• Turn right out of Blackwell Common car park and go straight over the crossroads in Blackfield; turn right on the B3053 (1¼ miles). There is a car park at Calshot (2¼ miles, pay-and-display) and more parking along the spit itself (pay-and-display, at SU 486017).

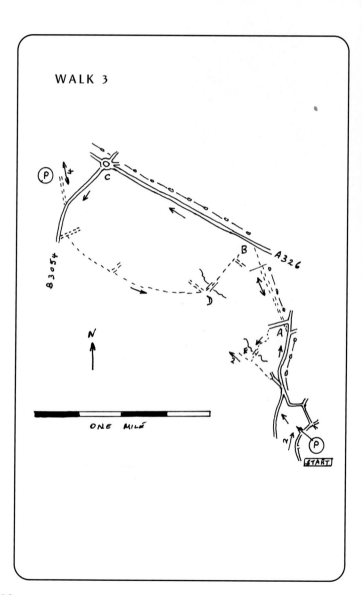

WALK 3

P

C

A326

B3054

B

D

N

A

E

ONE MILE

P

START

WALK 3: HOLBURY TO DIBDEN INCLOSURE

DISTANCE 5¼ miles (2¼ miles). Note that Walk 4 is quite short; if combined with this one the total is 7¾ miles.

PARKING At Holbury Manor Park in the small car park opposite Deepdene Close (SU 430036).

From the A326 (Totton to Fawley): pass through Holbury towards Fawley and take the right fork at the roundabout (7¾ miles from the A35, s.p. Blackfield); turn right at the traffic lights (⅓ mile, Rollestone Road). Take the 4th right (¾ mile, Foxcroft Drive) and turn left into the car park (¼ mile).

From the west: go through Beaulieu on the B3054 (s.p. Hythe); turn right by The Royal Oak (1 mile, s.p. Holbury – don't turn right again to Exbury). Pass The Bridge Tavern (1¼ miles), take the 2nd left (¼ mile, Foxcroft Drive) and turn left into the car park (¼ mile).

The boundary here follows the western fringes of Holbury and Hardley before a straight mile between Fawley Inclosure and the main road. The return leg of the walk is round the back of the inclosure, then by way of Holbury Mill Pond (E). Because the alternative would be a longish detour to avoid the swamp at the head of Dark Water, a half-mile section in the middle is used in both directions; unfortunately it is the bit by the industrial estate, but it is well screened and it only takes a few minutes to pass it by.

The strip of land beside the A326 Hythe Bypass (B to C) is screened by a thick hedge and fairly wide; if you want to get further from the road you will find a broad path among the trees near by on the left, although wet ground will send you back towards the road for a short way. This stretch is followed by the line of electricity pylons from Fawley Power Station and, surprisingly, you hardly notice them – the conductors are high overhead and the pylons well spaced; they are also impressively big when you stand at the bottom of one. At the end (C) you can look back

The latest model

along the straight mile and get a sense of achievement out of proportion to the effort of traversing it.

As for pubs, The Heath is across the roundabout (C – there is a handy stile in the corner) and you return past The Old Mill Inn.

Directions

From the car park bear leftish across the grass (**Walk 2** *joins here*) and find a gap in the trees leading to the pond (200 yds). Turn left to the gate and turn right in Park Lane (50 yds). Turn left at the junction (200 yds) and pass the sign for The Old Mill Inn. At the entrance to the mobile home park (A, ¼ mile), bear left on the bridleway (concrete track to start with) to the strip of open land beside the bypass (B, ⅓ mile). Go straight on parallel to the road.

When the fence curves left and bars your way (C, 1 mile) turn left along it and follow the road to the cattle grid. *For **Walk 4** cross the road to Dibden Inclosure car park.* Otherwise, stay on the road (**Walk 4** *returns here*), turn left on a gravel track (300 yds) then

turn right on a broad path (100 yds); follow it, eventually beside trees, as it curves left down to Hardley Bridge (D, 1 mile) which crosses another swampy valley feeding Dark Water.

Cross the bridge, go up the hill, turn right to the pylon (B, ½ mile), bear right to the gate (100 yds) and return along the bridleway. Cross the residential road (The Mill Pond) then immediately turn right along the edge of the mobile home park (A, ½ mile). Turn left on the path between fences (200 yds), follow it down through woods to Holbury Mill Pond (E, ¼ mile) and go ahead to the path just beyond the bridge.

*To rejoin **Walk 2** turn right.* Otherwise turn sharp left (not up the hill) and turn right up the lane by The Old Mill Inn (¼ mile). Turn right at the top (200 yds), take the first right (50 yds, Park Lane) enter the gate on the left to the pond (200 yds), turn right through the trees then bear left to the car park (200 yds).

Near by

Ashlett Creek (2¾ miles) is a short inlet on the south-western shore of Southampton Water. It hosts a number of yachts and small boats, and The Jolly Sailor pub. The large brick building is an old tide mill and granary of 1818, now used by the refinery employees' club. A short stroll along the far side of the creek leads to the shore of Southampton Water itself, a good place to view passing ships. At this point you are more or less opposite the mouth of the River Hamble, 1½ miles away.

• Turn right out of the car park, turn left at the T-junction (¼ mile), go straight over the traffic lights (¾ mile), turn left at the T-junction (½ mile), turn right at the T-junction on to the B3053 (¼ mile); take the 3rd left (½ mile – s.p. Jolly Sailor) then turn right (150 yds) to Ashlett Creek (½ mile, SU 466032).

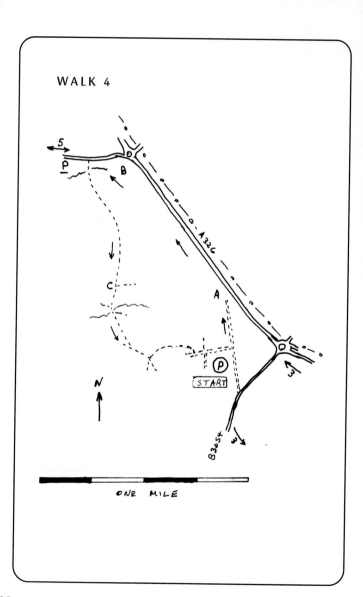

WALK 4

ONE MILE

WALK 4: DIBDEN INCLOSURE TO APPLEMORE

DISTANCE 2½ miles (1¼ miles); combined with Walk 5, the total is 8 miles.

PARKING Dibden Inclosure car park (SU 406057).

From the A326 (Totton to Fawley): turn on to the B3054 (5½ mile from the A35, s.p. Beaulieu); turn right by the cattle grid (¼ mile) the car park (200 yds).

From the west: go through Beaulieu on the B3054 towards Hythe; turn left by the cattle grid (2½ miles) to the car park (200 yds).

This trip round Dibden Inclosure is quite short, and if you choose not to combine it with one of the adjacent walks it would make a suitable outing for a summer evening or a winter afternoon. Don't leave it too late into the dusk though, because the last half-mile is in woodland. The walk starts near Dibden Purlieu. You will come across this quaint type of name again; a 'purlieu' is an area that was at one time within the Forest, and later excluded from it, or 'disafforested'.

The itinerary is similar to the second part of Walk 3, going outwards along the boundary between the trees and the road, and returning round the back of the inclosure. The straight mile doesn't seem as long because of the drop down Horestone Hill, and again you can find a path among the trees for part of the way. You have left Dark Water behind; the streams here flow westward to join the Beaulieu River.

The hill on the return leg (C), although only about 100 ft, has enough elevation to provide a westward vista across Beaulieu Heath, broader than usual in the Forest, and a view north-east to Southampton. To the north the pylons disappear behind Marchwood Inclosure (Walk 5).

Directions

Walk 3 joins here. Continue up the gravel road beside the car park (there is a gate in the corner) to emerge on to the broad sward between the trees and the road (A, ¼ mile). As you approach the last pylon before the roundabout (B, ¾ mile), bear left on a grassy avenue through the trees which cuts off the corner and avoids entanglement with a stream (although this route too can be boggy in places). Turn left beside the stream to the footbridge (¼ mile). *For Walk 5 cross the footbridge to the road.*

Turn left (*Walk 5 returns here*) and follow the broad path to the top of the hill (C, ½ mile). Go straight on, cross the footbridge below (200 yds), and turn left up the hill.

At the top (200 yds) keep left on a path just within the trees which follows the top of the valley side, occasionally dropping down a little to cross tributaries. Turn left on the gravel track (¼ mile) then turn right at the T-junction (300 yds) to the car park. *To return to Walk 3 go past the car park to the road (300 yds), and turn right.*

Near by

Train spotters will have their own ideas about what to do at **Beaulieu Road station** (4¾ miles), but it is recommended because it is reached by a short but scenic drive, and you may be interested to see the place where the pony sales are held (see 'Ponies and Other Matters', pages 166–7); the sale pens can

be surveyed from the railway bridge. It's a pleasant starting point for a short stroll, or a visit to The Beaulieu Road pub.

- From Dibden Inclosure car park turn left to the roundabout (¼ mile) then left again on the A326. At the next roundabout (1¼ miles) turn left. Go straight over the crossroads and continue to the junction with the B3056 (3 miles). Turn right to the car park (350 yds, opposite the pub, SU 351063).

A spring hedgerow

ORIGINS

The New Forest lies in the Hampshire Basin, a downfold in the chalk of southern England. Since its formation, the rise and fall of the land relative to sea level have resulted in a variety of sedimentary deposits, and as the New Forest slopes gently southwards a series of these layers is revealed, from the gravel cap on the northern plateau to various beds of sands and clays ranging to the Solent coast. The more fertile lands are in the south, but for the most part nutrients leach away readily, leaving poor soil. About 10,000 years ago, as temperatures recovered from the last Ice Age, the plants of our temperate climate colonised the land and the woodland became established.

It was not until the Late Stone Age that farming was invented; little evidence of Stone Age activity has been found in the New Forest, but there are the remains of well over a hundred burial mounds from the Bronze Age, and it was Bronze Age people who brought this new knowledge to the area. Starting about 4,000 years ago, they cleared patches of woodland, grew crops and grazed their animals. At that time, though, nothing was known about the fertility of the land; growing and harvesting crops removes nutrients from the soil which gradually becomes less fertile. Later the problem was dealt with by schemes of crop rotation, and today we use fertilisers, but Bronze Age people had a much simpler solution; when a patch of land became unproductive, they just cleared another patch of woodland and moved on to that, gradually creating the large tracts of open land still characteristic of the New Forest today. Once the soil is deprived of its natural tree cover and exposed to the elements, the rains leach out more nutrients and wash soil away, the land becomes even more impoverished and is colonised by the plants characteristic of the acid soils of heathland — particularly coarse grasses, heather (which gives the heathland its name), gorse (furze) and bracken.

Even in such conditions, the natural woodland will gradually regenerate, and the fact that it has not done so is taken to indicate that the area has been continually used for grazing animals. In the Iron Age people otherwise found little use for this land, even though there were important settlements in the Christchurch area, and there are several Iron Age hill forts on the western fringes of the New Forest above the fertile Avon Valley. Nor has any evidence of Roman settlement been discovered, although archaeologists have found the remains of Romano-British potteries — 'New Forest Ware' has been found widely distributed. By the end of the Saxon period, the area known as Ytene — meaning 'land of the Jutes' — is thought to have been characterised by scattered hamlets dependent on grazing and the resources of the residual woodland. At the time of the Norman Conquest it had probably changed little since the Bronze Age.

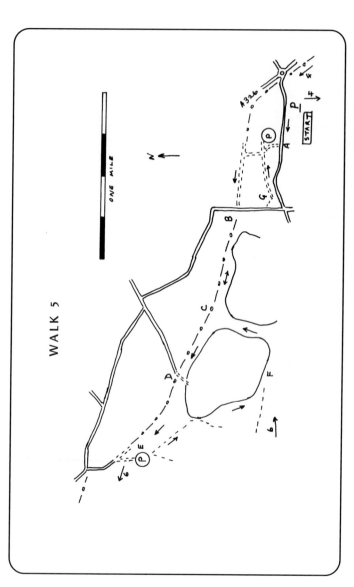

WALK 5

ONE MILE

N

WALK 5: APPLEMORE TO LONGDOWN

DISTANCE 5½ miles (2½ miles).

PARKING On the verge at SU 396073, or you can use the car park in Marchwood Inclosure at SU 392074 (A) and miss the first ¼ mile of the walk.

From the A326 (Totton to Fawley): turn off at the Applemore round-about (4¼ miles from the A35, s.p. Beaulieu Road station) then park on the left just after the cattle grid (250 yds).

From Beaulieu: take the B3054 (s.p. Hythe). Turn left at the round-about on to the A326 (3 miles) and left again at the next round-about (1 mile). Park on the left just after the cattle grid (250 yds).

From Lyndhurst: take the A35 towards Southampton then turn right on the B3056 (200 yds, s.p. Beaulieu). Pass Beaulieu Road station and turn left (3½ miles). Go straight over the crossroads (2 miles, s.p. Hythe) and park on the right just before the cattle grid (⅔ mile).

After two miles in the company of the main road and electricity pylons the forest boundary turns west and the surroundings become more rural. There is some retracing of steps for about ⅔ mile (B to C) because the Beaulieu River and enclosed land around Ipley Manor conspire between them to prevent an alternative return without a long detour (or a pair of waders).

Be warned that parts of this walk can be very muddy in winter. The dodgy bit on the western edge of Ipley Inclosure (approaching F) has been much improved recently, and the worst part is the repeated stretch (B to C). Walking boots will cope with it, but it can be tiresome, with much casting about for a passable route. Those who prefer not to leave it for a drier season, or to take to the road from Hanger Corner Farm to Foxhill Farm (B to D – passing The Bold Forester on the way), will find better going for parts of the way among the trees to the left. The problem is caused by hooves, primarily here of cattle, but we should remember that without grazing animals the Forest would not be what it is; indeed, it probably would not be here for us to enjoy at all.

Directions

Walk 4 joins here. Walk west along the road (away from the cattle grid) and turn right (A, ¼ mile) to Marchwood Inclosure car park. Follow the track up to the top and turn left (150 yds), then first right (50 yds). Go through the gate at the bottom (200 yds) and turn left. At the road (¼ mile) turn left, cross the cattle grid, then turn right beside the fence (B, 50 yds).

Cross the track by Foxhill Farm (D, 1 mile) and follow the footpath up the hill, keeping the fence in sight on the right, to Longdown car park (E, ½ mile). *Walk 6 starts here.*

Turn left through the car park then take the path which bears left, heading south-east towards the hills of the Isle of Wight, to the fence of Ipley Inclosure (½ mile). Turn right by the fence and follow it round the inclosure. As you walk down the slope, look out for a distant glimpse to your right (west) of a white house on a hillside; the eagle-eyed will pick out the spire of Lyndhurst church a little to the left, 4 miles away. *Walk 6 rejoins at F.* Keep sight of the fence on the left and find the culvert which allows you to cross a ditch (1 mile) and go ahead to the fence (C, 100 yds – be careful of your direction here, it is easy to get confused). Turn right and retrace the outward route by following the fence to the road (B, ⅔ mile).

Turn right on the road, then left on the path up the hill (300 yds). At the top, overlooking Ipley crossroads (G, 150 yds) turn left on the track through the inclosure. Take the first right (¼ mile) through the car park to the road (A, 150 yds) and turn left to return to the start near the cattle grid (¼ mile). *To rejoin **Walk 4** turn right and cross the footbridge.*

Ipley Inclosure

Scots pine near Longdown

Near by

Hythe (2 miles) is a pleasantly old-fashioned village on the shore of Southampton Water, which somehow contrives to seem both busy and peaceful at the same time; the centre has a surprising variety of shops. The church was built in 1874. For a small fee you can walk along the pier, which is ⅓ mile long and provides the embarkation point for the ferry to Southampton; it is served by the world's oldest pier railway. Southampton Water is about 1½ miles wide here; directly opposite is Weston Shore.

Hythe Marina is a short walk away and has a good view across Southampton Water to the berth used by *Queen Elizabeth II* and *Queen Mary II* when they are in port.

• Return to the A326 and go straight over the roundabout, following signs for Hythe, then Town Centre, then to one of the car parks (SU 424080).

WALK 6: LONGDOWN TO DEERLEAP

DISTANCE 3½ miles (¾ mile); combined with Walk 7, the total is 5¼ miles.

PARKING Longdown car park (SU 362087).

From the A35 (Ashurst to Totton): Turn south into Deerleap Lane (s.p. Longdown – 1 mile from Ashurst, ⅓ mile from the A326). Pass Deerleap car park (Walk 7) and turn right just after the post box (1¾ miles); the lane leads to Longdown car park (¼ mile).

From the south: take the A326 towards Totton; after the round-about with the B3054 (from Beaulieu) cross two more roundabouts then take the second left (3¾ miles, Staplewood Lane); turn right at the T-junction (1 mile), then first left (½ mile) to Longdown car park (¼ mile).

The short stretch of the boundary on the outward section connects two popular car parks. The return leg follows a popular walk before turning away to a quiet and secluded heath beside the infant Beaulieu River where the rest of the world could be a hundred miles away. The finish is a brisk pull uphill on a good path. Note that in winter much of the return leg (B to D) can be very wet underfoot and has two streams to cross which can be tricky – the second one especially – and you will have to cast about a bit for a dry passage. The same can be true for the route used for the return to Walk 5.

For about half a mile (B to C) the walk follows the railway (see Walk 25); Williford Cottages (B) is the site of accommodation built for the gatekeepers of the railway crossing – now a bridge. If you are curious to see what is on the other side, either cross the bridge here or cross the river at the footbridge (C) to the underbridge at Fulliford Passage, which is about half a mile north of Beaulieu Road station.

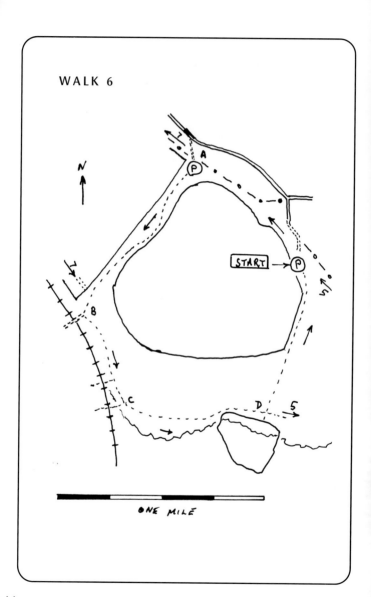

WALK 6

ONE MILE

Directions

Walk 5 joins here. Cut across to the trees and turn right (50 yds – on the right as you drove in – note that some of the Longdown Inclosure fence has been removed recently, so there may be more to go). Over the brow, follow the path across the shallow valley, including a right-then-left on the next brow, to Dear Leap car park (A, ¾ mile, *Walk 7 starts here*).

Turn left and follow the path between the two inclosures. At the approach to the railway bridge turn left (B, 1 mile, *Walk 7 rejoins here*). Follow the railway line (but don't drop down to the wet ground at the lineside; a path soon materialises) to Fulliford Passage (C, ½ mile) where a footbridge on the right indicates that the Beaulieu River has insinuated itself between the path and the railway. From here you may choose to follow the river bank for some of the way, although puddles and prickly trees may drive you back either the indistinct path beside the trees or to the main path 50 yds across the heather. You will come to a good path emerging from the gate of Decoy Pond Farm (D, ¾ mile).

Withycombe Shade

*To return to **Walk 5**, go straight on along a path about 100 yds to the left of the trees until the heath narrows to about 100 yds wide (²⁄₃ mile), then follow the fence on the left.* Otherwise, turn left up the hill to the car park (¾ mile).

Near by
The path from the back of **King's Hat** car park (3¾ miles) leads in a couple of minutes to a substantial footbridge over the Beaulieu River as it slides peacefully through its woodland glade. If you've changed out of your boots you'll find the ground is a bit muddy for extensive explorations, but if the weather has been fairly dry go straight on for about ¼ mile to a low plateau covered by a broad lawn. This is Gurnetfields Furzebrake – worth a visit for the name alone. Alternatively, when you come out of the trees turn right on a good path as far as a stream, then find your way back through the trees.

• From the car park, return to the road (¼ mile) and turn right. Turn right at the T-junction (1¼ mile, s.p. Ipley Cross) and pass The Bold Forester. Go straight over Ipley Cross (1¼ miles, s.p. Beaulieu) then turn right into The King's Hat car park (1 mile, SU 386055).

Deerleap Inclosure

WALK 7: DEERLEAP TO ASHURST

DISTANCE 3¾ miles (1¼ miles).

PARKING Deerleap car park (SU 353095 – note that there was no sign for this car park at my last visit)

From the A35 (Ashurst to Totton): Turn south into Deerleap Lane (s.p. Longdown – 1 mile from Ashurst, ⅓ mile from the A326. Turn right into the track just after the entrance to the Otter and Owl Park (1 mile).

From the south: take the A326 towards Southampton; after the roundabout with the B3054 (from Beaulieu) cross two more roundabouts then take the second left (3¾ miles, Staplewood Lane); turn right at the T-junction (1 mile), pass the turn for Longdown car park (Walk 6,½ mile) and turn left into the track just after the sign for the Otter and Owl Park (½ mile).

This is the walk on which you begin to feel you are getting somewhere. You have covered about 12 miles of the New Forest boundary and, for the first time, you arrive at a village with shops and one of the main roads across the Forest. Those doing the walk at a stretch and in need of shops will find them to the right; they include a post office, a general store and takeaways. There are two pubs – The Happy Cheese is near by, and The New Forest Hotel is over the railway bridge.

Much of the walk is in woodland inclosures; train spotters will enjoy the first half-mile of the return leg before covering a mile or so in Deerleap Inclosure.

Ashurst owes its existence to the Southampton and Dorchester railway (see Walk 25), which built a station to serve Lyndhurst (and which was until recently called 'Lyndhurst Road'). It was a popular destination for tourists in the nineteenth century, and businesses grew up around it – The New Forest Hotel was originally The Railway Hotel. Much of the residential development took place in the 1920s and although the name is an old one, the village itself did not become generally

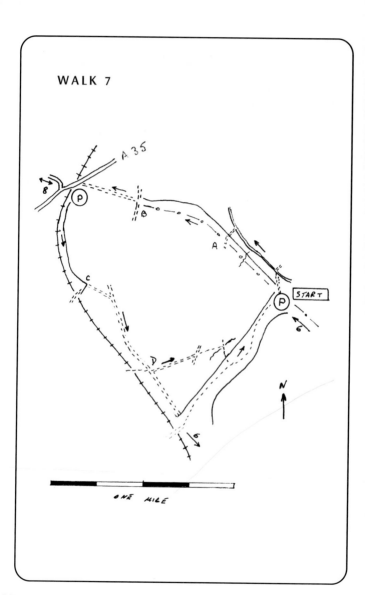

WALK 7

A.35

START

ONE MILE

48

known as Ashurst until the 1930s. The oldest building is thought to be the keeper's cottage (B) by Church Place Inclosure, built in 1810. The hospital, by the car park, was built in the 1830s as a workhouse.

Directions

Walk 6 joins here. Return across the cattle grid and immediately turn left. Go through the first gate on the left (200 yds) and turn right on the path by the fence (making detours where necessary to avoid prickly bits), passing a gate on the right (A, ¼ mile). At the cottage with a stag's head on the wall (B, ½ mile) turn right through the gate, then left.

At the car park by the gate of Ashurst Hospital (¼ mile, *Walk 8 starts here*) turn left (*Walk 8 rejoins here*) and go through gate on the left (100 yds) shortly before the railway line (don't take the path right at the end, which leads only to the station).

As you approach trees ahead bear left through the gate (C, ½ mile). At the first junction in the track (300 yds) turn right.

At the next junction (D, ½ mile) return to **Walk 6** *by going straight on to leave the inclosure through the gate (¼ mile)*. Otherwise turn left. Go straight over a crossing (¼ mile) and turn right over a footbridge by a T-junction (300 yds). Leave the inclosure by the gate (150 yds) and turn left to return to the car park (½ mile).

Near by

Eling (3¾ miles) is beside the creek at the mouth of Bartley Water as it flows into the upper reach of estuary of the Test. For a 15-minute stroll, turn right out of the car park and go up the hill to the church, which is of various dates from Saxon times onwards and much restored in the nineteenth century. Just past the church take the gate on the left into the graveyard and follow the path down to Goatee Shore beside the estuary, almost opposite the container terminal. Follow the shore path left to return to the car park. To extend the walk, cross the toll

Pannage (see page 167).

bridge, pass The Tide Mill, and turn right to The Anchor pub.

•   From the car park return to the road and turn left. Turn right on the A35 (1 mile) and follow the brown signs for The Tide Mill as follows: turn right at the second roundabout on to the A326 (1¼ miles). Turn left at the traffic lights (½ mile) then second left (½ mile). Pass the church and turn left into the car park at the bottom of the hill (½ mile, SU 366124).

WALK 8: ASHURST TO NICHOLAS CORNER

DISTANCE 5½ miles (2½ miles); combined with walk 9, the distance is 8½ miles.

PARKING Ashurst car park (SU 334013) on the south side of the A35, just east of the railway bridge (s.p. Hospital).

Turn off the main road opposite the petrol station, then turn right to the car park.

The outward journey follows the boundary in woodland, with occasional patches of lawn; the return is by way of field paths just outside the Forest. There are two pubs in Ashurst (see Walk 7), and for those to whom 5½ miles without refreshment is too much of an ordeal, there is The Gamekeeper in Woodlands (E) on the return journey.

For simplicity, the directions below follow the road for the first half mile; if you prefer to find your way through the wood, enter the first gate on the left (100 yds after the bend) then find a sketchy path not too far from the road; on the return leg, go straight across the road at A and turn left after 100 yds.

Directions

Walk 7 joins here. Cross the main road, turn left over the railway bridge, then right into Woodlands Road (100 yds). Enter the inclosure through the 3rd gate on the left (A, ½ mile). Follow the track to the T-junction (⅓ mile). Turn right, cross the bridge, and follow the track until it turns away right (¼ mile); go straight ahead through the gate (200 yds).

Continue in more or less the same direction to Busketts Wood car park (B, ½ mile – if in doubt, err to the right where the road will guide you).

Go straight on to the track ahead which skirts trees on the right (if you came along from the road, take the right fork – s.p. Cottage

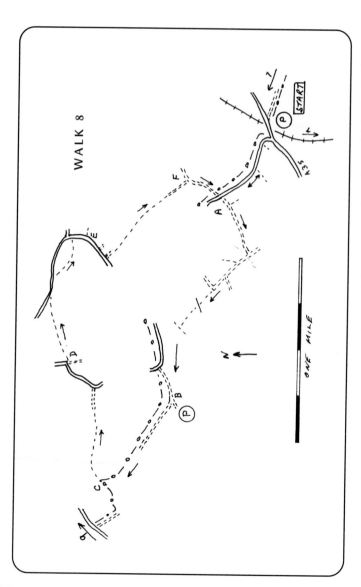

WALK 8

ONE MILE

Only). When the track turns off to a house (⅓ mile) go straight on, keeping the fence on your right and dodging round holly as necessary until the fence bears away to the right (¼ mile). Go straight ahead until cottages or another fence bar your way (C, 100 yds).

*For **Walk 9** turn left, turn right on the track (100 yds) and right again on the road (300 yds).* Otherwise turn right and go through the gate on the right (100 yds, ***Walk 9*** *rejoins here*). After a muddy start the path soon turns into a good track leading to Bartley Road at Goldenhayes (½ mile). Turn left.

Where the road turns sharp left (D, ¼ mile, at the sign for Rossiters Lane) turn right on to the track then immediately left on what becomes a path between fences. Turn right on the road (⅓ mile) then turn right on to the footpath (150 yds – note: if this path is still choked with nettles, stay on the road and take the first right).

At Woodlands Road (¼ mile) turn right, pass The Gamekeeper (E) and a thatched house; just before the next thatched roof (¼ mile), turn left on a footpath (look back to see the sign). Turn right at the end (F, ⅔ mile) on the unsurfaced road. At the junction with

Fly agaric

Woodlands Road (A, 300 yds) turn left to the A35, turn left across the railway bridge, then turn right and right again to the car park (½ mile). *To return to* **Walk 7** *continue through the car park towards the railway line.*

Near by

Lyndhurst (2½ miles) is 'the capital of the New Forest'. The name means 'lime tree wood', and was recorded in the Domesday Book as *Linhest*. It has a Visitor Centre and the New Forest Museum, a selection of shops – antiques and souvenirs being well represented – and a variety of places of refreshment, licensed and otherwise. The church, standing high above the village, was completed in 1869 and is well worth a visit if you like Victorian architecture, both for

Busketts Lawn Inclosure

the building itself and for the interior decoration, carving and stained glass by various eminent artists of the day. Round the back, planted with roses, is the grave of Alice Hargreaves, *née* Liddell, the inspiration for 'Alice' in Lewis Carroll's *Alice's Adventures in Wonderland*. Queen's House, mostly seventeenth-century but of earlier origins, is the local headquarters of the Forestry Commission, and includes the Verderers' Hall.

For a short exploration, turn right out of the car park then left on the main road. The Visitor Centre and museum are beside the main car park (turn left just before the Working Men's Club – s.p. Library). The church is at the top of the High Street on the left, and

Queen's House is just beyond. Back at the car park there are pleasant views from the hill near by which you can enjoy from the comfort of seats in the shade of yews.

• From Ashurst, turn left out of the car park on to the A35. Turn left on the B3056 (2½ miles, s.p. Beaulieu) then immediately left again into Boltons Bench car park (SU 303082); if busy, there is extra parking beyond the War Memorial. This car park is recommended rather than the one in the centre of the village because it avoids entanglement with the busy one-way system at the cost of a two-minute walk. On leaving at busy times, find a way home through Ashurst or Beaulieu.

WILLIAM I

In the Middle Ages, nothing – people, goods or news – moved over-land faster than walking pace. In order for the king to keep in touch with events and maintain his rule it was necessary for him to travel around and visit his barons from time to time. The whole court travelled with him – family, servants, administrators, lawyers, no doubt a variety of hangers on, and a body of soldiers to deal with any trouble. They all went traipsing round the countryside on what was known as the 'Royal Progress'. The king could not land up on a baron's doorstep and expect him to be able to feed this lot; indeed, its arrival disrupted local markets, so it was necessary for him to make his own provision. Hunting reserves were established for the exclusive use of the Crown to provide venison – the meat of the deer and boar – in the uncultivated land where the wild animals were to be found.

In late Saxon times there were royal hunting reserves in England and a more formal system in northern France which William I imported and strengthened by creating a body of strict legislation to regulate them. The purpose of this 'Forest Law' was to protect the wild animals and their habitat; it specified what people could and could not do, who would supervise and administer it, and the penalties for transgression. The system grew to include about a hundred royal forests all over England, such as Sherwood, Kesteven, Savernake, Mendip and Windsor; at one time whole counties, for example Essex and Berkshire, came under the Forest Law.

Although the royal forests were usually based on land to which the Crown had some claim, their boundaries often extended beyond it, restricting what landowners could do even on their own land. They were not allowed to cut down trees, put up fences or convert the 'waste' to farmland, nor of course to hunt the wild animals. The value of land that fell under Forest Law was much reduced. The penalties were harsh, including blinding and mutilation (William II introduced the death penalty for killing the king's deer). Lesser offences were punished by fines or confiscation of property; a smallholder losing his land in this way was deprived of his livelihood.

In administering the law, offenders were brought first before the Woodmote. If this court decided there was a case to answer, the accused was referred to the Court of Swainmote and Attachment, which dealt with the lesser offences and referred the more serious ones to the Court of Justices in Eyre, a peripatetic court which visited every three years.

People who had traditionally used the open land to graze their animals were allowed to continue, subject to the withdrawal of their stock during the winter months to remove competition with the deer when fodder was scarce ('winter heyning') and during the 'fence month' in midsummer to avoid disturbing them while they gave birth to their young.

Thus was established the forest system. The word 'forest' came from Norman French meaning 'land not enclosed for agriculture' and it was used to refer to land that was subject to the Forest Law. Since much of this land was the natural woodland, it is not surprising that in latter days the word 'forest' has come to mean a large area of woodland.

WALK 9

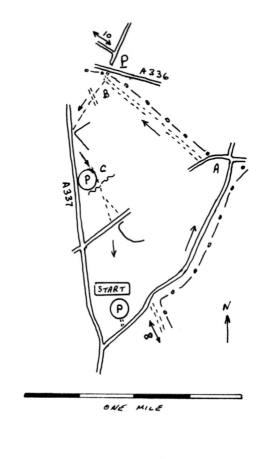

ONE MILE

58

WALK 9: BROCKISHILL
TO CADNAM

DISTANCE 2¾ miles (1½ miles). Combined with Walk 10, the total is 7¾ miles.

PARKING Brockishill Green car park (SU 299118).

From Cadnam (M27 junction 1): take the A336 (s.p. Cadnam); at the next roundabout take the A337 (s.p. Lyndhurst). Take the second left (1¼ miles) and turn left into the car park (200 yds).

From Lyndhurst: take the A337 towards Cadnam. Take first right after leaving the village (2 miles) and turn left into the car park (200 yds).

Today you come to another milestone as you reach Cadnam. Allow yourself a bit of poetic license and say you have completed the eastern boundary by calling next three walks 'The North East Corner'. As with the previous walk, the scenery is relatively domestic – woods and fields, and more holly to negotiate on the return leg. As you walk the first mile along the quiet lane of Brockishill Road to Bartley, you can ponder whether by selling the yacht, giving up smoking and sending the children up chimneys, you really could afford one of the comfortable looking cottages.

There are three pubs in Cadnam, all within 5 minutes. The directions for Walk 10 will take you to The White Hart and The Sir John Barleycorn; for The Coach and Horses turn right on the A336 at B.

Directions

From the car park turn left along Brockishill Road. Pass the point where **Walk 8** joins (¼ mile) and turn left at the crossroads by Bartley Post Office (A, ¾ mile) into Beechwood Road.

Immediately after the cattle grid (200 yds), take the bridleway on the right; it is a good track with a short stretch of path about half way along. At the end (B, ½ mile) *turn right over the cattle grid for* **Walk 10** *and cross the road to The Parade*, otherwise turn left

Bartley

(**Walk 10** *rejoins here*) and follow the path uphill through woods, crossing the drive of Bartley Lodge Hotel, to the main road (¼ mile).

Turn left inside the fence to Cadnam Cricket car park (C, 200 yds). Go straight on, keeping the cricket field near by on the left, head for a gap in the trees ahead and cross the stream (200 yds). Go straight up the hill, taking the right fork half way up, and cross the road (300 yds).

Now test your sense of direction – the car park is ⅓ mile straight ahead through woodland. With a compass, head south; if in doubt, err to the right where the main road will prevent you straying too far. When you finally decide you are completely lost

among holly bushes, the car park is about 200 yards away. If you miss it and come to Brockishill Road, turn right; if this brings you to the cattle grid by the A337, you were nearer than you thought, and should have turned left.

*To return to **Walk 8**, go left along the road then turn right on the track just beyond the wood, at a sign for Forest Glade House (¼ mile). Turn left after the cottages (300 yds) then find the gate on the right (100 yds).*

Near by

Minstead (2 miles) is a small, quiet village where The Trusty Servant public house and the village shop overlook the green. Turn left in front of the pub to visit the church, which in contrast with Lyndhurst (Walk 8) is an unpretentious, homely place where it is easy to imagine the community assembling for its weekly get-together. It has an unusual three-decker pulpit, placed on an inside corner where everybody can see it. At the far end of the graveyard, under an oak and marked by a substantial stone cross, is the grave of Sir Arthur Conan Doyle, creator of Sherlock Holmes.

• Turn right out of the car park then turn left on the A337 (300 yds). Take the first right (¾ mile, s.p. Minstead, note: you come upon this turn suddenly on the brow of the hill). At the village green (1¼ miles) there is a small parking area to the right (SU 282110); there is also room for a few cars by the church – turn left in front of the pub.

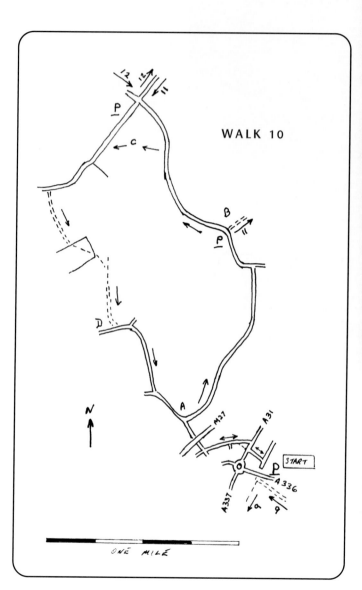

WALK 10

ONE MILE

62

WALK 10: CADNAM TO CROCK HILL

DISTANCE 5 miles (1¾ miles).

PARKING In The Parade at Cadnam (SU 297135).

From Cadnam (M27 junction 1): take the A336 and go straight over the next roundabout (s.p. A336 Totton); turn left by the telephone box (200 yds) and park in the service road.

In most of the New Forest you are free to wander at will, either on the open heath, or in the woodland inclosures. Between Cadnam and Nomansland there is more than the usual proportion of enclosed land, with few paths, so much of this walk is along public roads. They are, however, quiet country lanes, with little traffic, and a pleasure to tread; for the most part there are grass verges for those whose feet really do object to tarmac, although it does offer the advantage, indeed a welcome relief after wet weather, of being dry and firm underfoot.

The wide verges of Cadnam Lane (from A) open out after a mile to Cadnam Common and the road passes Crock Hill (B) which merits a few minutes exploration. It is a pleasant knoll, firm underfoot with a carpet of leaves, wooded with oak and holly, and presided over by two fine beeches; a quiet and peaceful place. Don't expect a view though, even in winter, because of the holly.

On the other hand, Stagbury Hill (C) with its triangulation pillar at 200 ft, is no Matterhorn but is at least high enough to see open views above the trees:

North: beyond the Furzley crossroads (¼ mile) is Dean Hill (6 miles) between Whiteparish and West Dean, on the ridge which runs westward to Pepperbox Hill (see 'Near by' on Walk 13).
West: the wooded hillside is Bramshaw Wood (2 miles, Walk 13).
South: the radio mast sticking above the trees like a strangled pine (2½ miles) is at the offices SSE Power Distribution (formerly Southern Electricity) at Malwood Castle near Minstead.

South-south-east: the hills are on the Isle of Wight (20 miles).
South-east: the village visible when the leaves have fallen is Newbridge (1 mile).
East: the tower blocks are at Redbridge (6 miles) on the western fringe of Southampton.

Physical and spiritual needs are catered for in The Parade where you park, which has an estate agent, a political party office, a feed merchant and, you may be pleased to hear since you have now completed 45 miles of the circular walks, a chiropodist. The post office is a few yards away (turn right on the main road), and there is a shop at the petrol station (turn right on the A31). You pass The White Hart and The Sir John Barleycorn, one of the oldest pubs in Hampshire.

Directions
Walk 9 joins here. Walk away from the main road up Old Lyndhurst Road and take the first left (30 yds, White Hart Lane). Go straight across the main road (200 yds, Romsey Road) and up the path beside The White Hart. Turn left on Old Romsey Road (50 yds) then turn right at the crossroads into Kewlake Lane (300 yds, or go straight on for the Sir John Barleycorn). Pass under the motorway bridge and turn right into Cadnam Lane (A, ¼ mile). At the T-junction with Furzley Road (1 mile) turn left.

Pass Crock Hill (B, ¼ mile, *Walk 11 starts here*) and climb Stagbury Hill on the left (C, ½ mile). *Walk 11 rejoins here. Walk 12 starts at the crossroads.*

Go down the other side of Stagbury Hill to the road (300 yds – aim for a cottage with two gables) and turn left (*Walk 12 rejoins here*). Take the footpath on the left (¼ mile), pass Blenmans Farm and go through the gate into the field at the bottom (¼ mile). Go straight ahead towards an oak and cross a stile on the left just before the gate in the corner (200 yds). Bear right, then right again on the grassy track, which leads through a gate to open heath (200 yds, Cadnam Common).

Looking towards Furzley from Stagbury Hill

Cadnam Common

Keep to the right and leave the common up a muddy lane. At the road (D, ¼ mile, Kewlake Lane) turn left. Pass the lane to Storm's Farm, and turn left at the junction by Manor Farm (½ mile).

Take the right fork at Cadnam Lane (A, 300 yds), pass under the motorway, turn left at the crossroads, turn right on the path beside The White Hart, cross the road into White Hart Lane and turn right at the T-junction to The Parade on the left (½ mile). *To return to* **Walk 9** *cross the main road to the short track and go straight on over the cattle grid.*

Near by

Rufus Stone (2½ miles) commemorates the death in 1100 of King William II – William Rufus. While hunting in the New Forest he was hit by an arrow shot by Sir Walter Tyrrell; it was supposedly an accident resulting from a ricochet, but enough people stood to gain from his death for there to have been many suggestions that he was in fact murdered. There is doubt too as to whether the stone, encased in a Victorian iron overcoat, marks the correct spot. More certain is that a good place to ponder such mysteries is The Sir Walter Tyrrell Inn, 250 yards further up the road.

• From Cadnam, turn right out of The Parade, go straight over the first roundabout and at the second (½ mile) turn left on the A31. Take the first right (1½ miles, s.p. Rufus Stone – note: this is a hairy manoeuvre involving a U-turn across fast traffic to the far lane, which acts as a slip road for what is now a left turn into the road you want). Turn right into the car park (¼ mile, SU 270125).

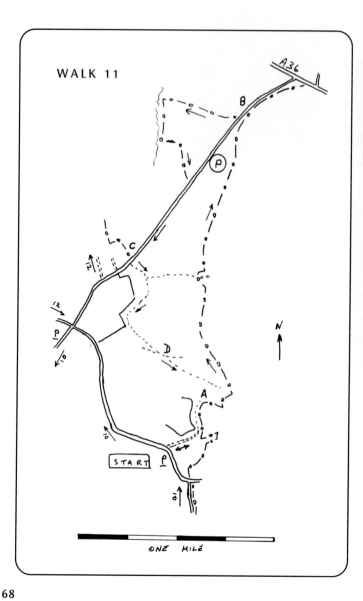

WALK 11

A36

START

ONE MILE

68

WALK 11: CROCK HILL TO FURZLEY

DISTANCE 5½ miles (¾ mile).

PARKING On the verge at Crock Hill (SU 295145) by a track on the north side of the road near a small National Trust sign.

From Telegraph Hill (see Walk 15): take the B3078 towards Cadnam. Take the second left (1¾ miles, s.p. Bramshaw). Cross the B3079 (1¼ miles), turn right at the Furzley crossroads (1 mile) and park on the verge near a track on the left (1 mile).

From Cadnam (M27 junction 1): take the A336 (s.p. Cadnam, Totton) then the first left (200 yds). Go straight over the crossroads, straight on at the next junction, pass under the motorway bridge and take the first right (¼ mile, Cadnam Lane). Turn left at the T-junction (1 mile, Furzley Road). Park on the verge near a track on the right (¼ mile).

Half Moon Common is a rising finger of land about a mile long which narrows to a point as it reaches out to touch the A36 near West Wellow. Like Cadnam Common, it is owned by the National Trust. The walk beside it seems a long steady climb, but the rise is only about 80 ft. The wooded hill over your left shoulder as you do so, about 2 miles south-west, is Bramshaw Wood (Walk 13). The common has a thick sprinkling of pine and birch, is mostly dry underfoot and softly carpeted; it is bounded by fenced plantations to the east and Blackhill Road on the west, and is no more than half a mile at the widest so you won't get lost if you don't stick to the route.

Towards the far end at Black Hill is an area of about 50 acres where the common crosses the road and drops down to the stream which separates it from the fields of Canada. You will probably meet a few strollers and dog walkers on the main part of the common, but down here you're unlikely to see a soul.

Directions

Walk 10 joins here. Walk along the track beside Crock Hill. After passing the farm to which it gives access, it narrows to a path; follow the fence on the right and cross a long footbridge then a short plank bridge (A, ⅓ mile). Move about 50 yds to the left to avoid wet ground; the fence returns to join you then turns left (200 yds) along the side of Half Moon Common. Follow it until you come to cottages on the left (B, 1¼ miles).

Cross to the cottages and come back down the road. When the fence curves away right, follow it down to the stream, turn left beside it, then let the fence bring you back towards the road. When you come to an acre of mud and hoofprints by a farm gate (1 mile) turn left uphill to the road, casting as far left as necessary for a dry crossing of the ditch. Turn right on the road to Furzley Cottage with its stacks of timber (C, ½ mile).

To continue to **Walk 12** *take the second track on the right (300 yds). To return to* **Walk 10** *keep going to the crossroads (⅓ mile) then bear left and climb the hill.* Otherwise, turn left over the nearby footbridge, ignore the footpath sign which points a bit to the left, and go straight ahead then bear slightly right on an indistinct path. Take a sandy path on the right climbing into woodland (250 yds).

Ignore the fence which joins you on the right before turning away again. When the path emerges from trees (D, ½ mile) and curves left of a low hill ahead (Duck Hill), turn right instead on a path which skirts the lower right hand slope of the hill; this brings you back to the fence (½ mile). Turn right to the footbridge (A, 200 yds) and follow the fence back to Crock Hill (½ mile, **Walk 12** *returns here*).

Near by

Romsey (7 miles) is an historic country town on the River Test, which was used as the setting for the Inspector Wexford television programmes. Its large abbey is a superb example of late Norman architecture, and not to be missed. On the edge of the town is

Half Moon Common

Broadlands, once the home of Palmerston and later of the Mountbattens. Romsey was the home of the former Strong's brewery (the brand has been revived locally in recent years), which was responsible for well-known signs informing travellers that 'You're in the Strong Country'.

• With your back to Crock Hill, turn left as if to Cadnam, but pass the right turn and go straight over the cattle grid (¼ mile). At the main road (¾ mile), turn left and follow signs for A3090 Romsey, then for the town centre car park (6 miles, SU 354211, pay-and-display). Go down one of the alleys at the back of the car park then turn left to the market square where the Lord Palmerston awaits at the start of your explorations.

Autumn colours on West Wellow Common

WALK 12: FURZLEY TO BARFORD FARMS

DISTANCE 4½ miles (3½ miles).

PARKING On the verge by the crossroads at Furzley (SU 286164).

From Cadnam (M27 junction 1): take the B3079 (s.p. Fordingbridge); pass the junction with the B3078 at Brook (1 mile) then take the first right (1 mile). Park just before the crossroads (1 mile).

From Telegraph Hill (see Walk 15): take the B3078 towards Cadnam. Take the second left (1¾ miles, s.p. Bramshaw). Cross the B3079 (1¼ miles) then park just before the crossroads (1 mile).

From the A36 (Salisbury to Southampton): turn south-west into Blackhill Road (s.p. Bramshaw – 13 miles from Salisbury, 2 miles from M27 junction 2); park on the verge just beyond the crossroads (1¾ miles).

After Half Moon Common (Walk 11), the other North Eastern protrusion is a mile-wide stretch of open heath comprising Canada, West Wellow, and Plaitford Commons. The land between is Canada, which provides for the inner self in two ways: you pass the Primitive Methodist Chapel (1906), the adjective presumably referring to the variety of religious practice rather than the architecture, and shortly afterwards the back gate of The Rockingham Arms.

At the northern end of the walk (A) is a triangulation pillar which, at 150 ft, is high enough to give pleasant views; it carries a small commemorative plaque and Ordnance Survey benchmark S2721. 'Trig points' such as this can be found all over the country, usually on high points for visibility, providing reference marks and convenient plinths for the surveyors' instruments. They are familiar landmarks and popular walkers' objectives, especially in hill country; sadly, the development of satellite mapping techniques has made them redundant, although some now carry signs indicating that they have a use in connection with the satellite Global Positioning System (GPS).

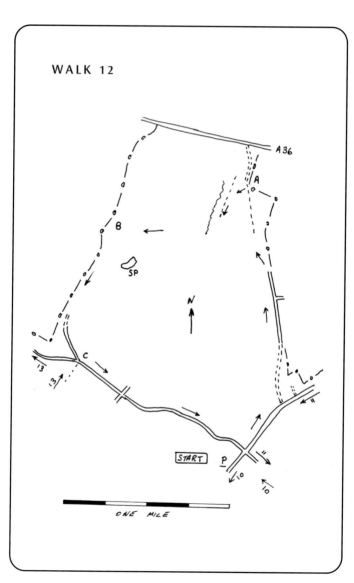

WALK 12

A 36

B

SP

N

13
13

C

START P

10
10
11

ONE MILE

74

On the western side of Plaitford Common (B), the New Forest boundary joins the county boundary, which it follows for the next 5 miles or so. Here you can lean over a gate with your feet in Hampshire and your head in Wiltshire. Also on Plaitford Common is Sturtmoor Pond (SP). If time permits, make the short detour to visit it; it is one of those places where a small stretch of water changes a nice spot into a lovely one.

Directions

Take the road north-east from the crossroads (past the phone box), then take the first track on the left (⅓ mile, **Walk 11 joins here**). The track soon acquires a tarmac surface; follow it to the end (1 mile). Bear left up the rise, then, keeping left of wet ground, follow the path you will see climbing the hill ahead to the triangulation pillar near a house (A, ½ mile).

Your next point of call is an electricity pylon (B) – the one at the angle of the line, west-south-west; if you lose track of which one it is, remember it's the one which, being at an angle, has the insulators pulled out sideways instead of hanging straight down. Trees, wet ground and a sluggish stream make a beeline unattractive, so go down the slope aiming for the end of the trees and pick up a path bearing left. When this peters out to an indistinct pony track, head straight for the pylon, casting about as far left as necessary for a way across the stream. On the brow of the hill, look left for a view of Sturtmoor Pond (SP); if you plan to visit it later, note its position well, because its not as easy to find as you might think. You should now see a path that leads to the pylon (B, 1 mile).

Follow the cables to the edge of the common, and turn left about 20 yds before a gate (80 yds). When the land opens out, follow the line of trees on the right, crossing a ditch on the right at the first opportunity (a plank bridge). Follow the fence into Deazle Wood and join a track leading to the road at Barford Farms (C, 1 mile).

For **Walk 13** turn right along the road to Lords Oak car park (½ mile). Otherwise, turn left (**Walk 13 rejoins here**) and follow the road across Penn Common to the Furzley crossroads (1 mile).

Sturtmoor Pond

*To return to **Walk 10** turn right; to return to **Walk 11** go straight on to Crock Hill (1 mile).*

Near by

With luck, you will find both cricket and golf to watch at **Round Hill** (2½ miles), or you can stroll in the peaceful tree-studded golf course landscape. Explorations across the road will be quieter – keep leftish for Brook Wood, a lovely area of mature beech and oak woodland; if you plan to go far, though, take your compass – it is

a confusing area. On either side of the road beware of soft ground in winter. Close by, in Brook, there are two pubs – The Bell and The Green Dragon.

• Leave Furzley crossroads going south-west (away from the phone box). Turn left on the B3079 (1¼ miles, s.p. Cadnam). At Brook, turn right on the B3078 (¾ mile, s.p. Fordingbridge). Ignore the sign at a private entry to Round Hill, and shortly turn left into the Round Hill car park (⅓ mile, SU 286141).

THE MIDDLE AGES

The forest system flourished for about 250 years. The Forest Law was designed to protect the deer and boar, and penalties included death for killing a deer and having the hands cut off for hunting; other measures included the requirement that anyone crossing the forest should unstring his bow. Dogs of a size sufficient for hunting were crippled by having their front claws removed – animals which had been 'lawed' or 'expeditated' in this way could still be used for herding cattle, and as guard dogs. To protect the habitat, offences included encroaching on the forest land, erecting structures or digging fishponds, cutting down trees and cultivation.

The Forest and its laws were administered by a variety of officials. The senior official was the Warden. Others included verderers, who were responsible for the 'vert' – the grass and foliage which provided fodder for the deer; they were usually knights and sat as judges in the court. Each area, or 'walk', of the Forest was managed by a forester; agisters administered the grazing and collected the associated fees, rangers drove deer back on to the forest from surrounding lands, and regarders reported to the court on the state of the Forest.

The system was much disliked, and in 1217, under pressure from the barons, Henry III produced the Charter of the Forest, which reduced the harsher penalties, switching the emphasis to fines, which were to become an important source of Crown revenue. It

defined, and thus limited, the powers of the officials, and pro-
tected the grazing and other rights of the commoners; it also
agreed to withdraw the extensions to the boundaries made by King
John, who had already agreed to do so in Magna Carta in 1215.
Later agreements provided for the disafforestation of extensions
by Richard I and Henry II; this agreement was eventually honoured
by Edward I and Edward III. In the case of the New Forest, the
boundary at the end of the thirteenth century remained more or
less unchanged until 1964. In the absence of maps, boundaries
were defined by walking round them; the boundary is still known
as 'the perambulation'.

From the start of the fourteenth century, there was a gradual
decline in the importance of the royal forests. Edward I introduced
a system of national taxation, making the revenues from the
forests less important, administration became less efficient, and
the justices visited less frequently to hold 'eyres'. The local courts
continued to record offences, and from time to time some king
would attempt to restore his finances after an expensive military
adventure by ordering a forest eyre. By the time of the Stuarts, the
forests had fallen into decay, and only two eyres were held during
the seventeenth century; Charles I was the last king to take significant quantities of venison from the royal forests.

WALK 13

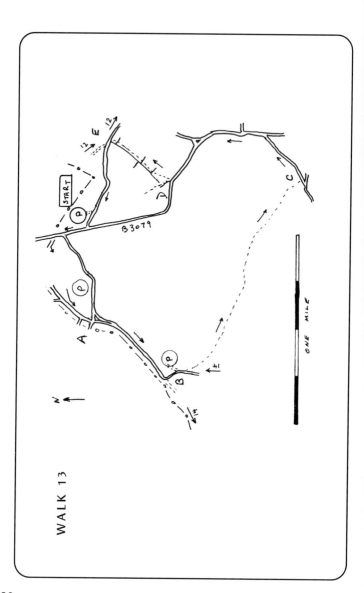

ONE MILE

80

WALK 13: LORD'S OAK
TO PIPERS WAIT

DISTANCE 4½ miles (1¼ miles).

PARKING Lord's Oak car park (SU 262174).

From the A36 (Salisbury to Southampton): turn south on to the B3079 at Landford (s.p. Bramshaw – 10 miles from Salisbury, 5 miles from M27 junction 2). After the cattle grid (1¾ miles) take the first left (300 yds) and turn left into the car park (50 yds).

From other directions: follow the directions for Walk 12 then turn left at the Furzley crossroads; the car park is on the right just before the junction with the B3079 (1¾ miles).

Since Stagbury Hill (Walk 10) you have had glimpses of the hanging woods above Bramshaw, which are said to have provided timber for the roofs of Salisbury Cathedral. This walk climbs beside them and returns along the top; when a gap in the trees gives a view north-east, look out for Plaitford Common (Walk 12) two miles away below. The electricity pylons are visible on a clear day; from here the useful corner pylon appears to be on the near end of the line.

In Nomansland (A) the green and the road are in Hampshire, but the houses are in Wiltshire; the postal address is 'near Salisbury', 12 miles away. It must be an odd feeling to have the county boundary right across your doorstep. The village acquired its name at a time when it was not clear whether it lay within the perambulation; the matter was settled in 1801, but the name remained. There is a Methodist chapel which replaced an earlier building in 1901, a restaurant and a pub, The Lamb. The little shelter on the green, with its timber frame and brick infill, is built over an old well; it is inscribed 'The Well of Sacrifice' and is dedicated as a War Memorial.

Bramshaw (C to D) also has a nonconformist chapel, dated 1883 and, surprisingly, a Rolls Royce dealer (leave your credit card at

Nomansland

home). The Church of St Peter (D) is the best part of a mile north of
the village, perhaps because it was common to build a church at
the centre of the parish it served rather than at a particular village.
It is an unusual and rather pleasant brick building elevated above
the road. Parts of it have survived from the thirteenth century, but
most of it dates from 1829. Before the boundary changes of 1895,
it was in the odd situation of having the nave in Wiltshire and the
chancel in Hampshire. Inside it turns out to be smaller than it looks
and has a charming intimacy. At the front of the church are two
large rhododendrons, one yellow, the other a glorious crimson.
Those who think that graveyards ought to be neat and tidy should
be persuaded to go round the back of the church in spring, when

the lower graveyard is a profusion of daffodils, bluebells (white ones as well as blue), wood anemones, and primroses – a timeless, gentle remembrance.

Directions

Walk 12 joins here. Turn right out of the car park, right again at the T-junction, pass a road on the left, then turn left on to the grass just before the cattle grid (300 yds). Make for the houses ahead, keeping well up the slope on the left to avoid wet ground. Turn left on the road (⅓ mile).

Follow the road through Nomansland (A), passing The Lamb on the right, and up the hill (there is easy going in the wood on your left) to a sharp left-hand bend near the top (⅔ mile). *For **Walk 14** go straight ahead on the track beside the fence.* Otherwise, follow the road round the left and right hand bends to Pipers Wait car park (B, 150 yds). Turn left off the road (but not back into the car park). ***Walk 14** returns here.*

Keep close to the top of the slope of Bramshaw Woods on your left. Don't let paths tempt you to lose height; stay on the highest ground as the ridge narrows. Shortly after you begin to feel lost it drops easily down to the road (C, 1¼ miles). Turn left.

Turn left at the next junction and follow the road through Bramshaw. Immediately before the church (D, 1 mile), turn right on the right hand of two footpaths (i.e. not the one through the side of the churchyard) following the direction of the sign diagonally

St Peter's, Bramshaw

across the field to a pair of oaks. Cross the stile and take the path along the edge of the fields to the road at Barford Farms (E, ⅓ mile). *To resume **Walk 12** turn right.* Otherwise turn left to return to the car park (½ mile).

Near by

At a little over 500 ft, **Pepperbox Hill** (6¼ miles) is an area rich in flora and fauna in the care of the National Trust. The 'Pepperbox' is a folly in the form of a small tower built in 1606; close by is a toposcope indicating the features of the view, the highlight of which is Salisbury, 5 miles away; when the sun catches the cathedral spire the effect is magical.

• Turn right out of the car park and right again at the T-junction on to the B3079. Turn left on the A36 (2 miles). Turn right on the brow of the hill into a narrow unsurfaced track (4½ miles, s.p. Pepperbox Hill), then turn right into the car park (100 yds, SU 212249). On departure, turning right on to the A36 is not recommended.

WALK 14: PIPERS WAIT TO TELEGRAPH HILL

DISTANCE 5¼ miles (1½ miles).

PARKING Pipers Wait car park (SU 249166).

From Cadnam (M27 junction 1): take the B3079 (s.p. Fordingbridge) then the left fork at Brook on to the B3078 (1 mile); take the second right (2 miles, s.p. Nomansland). The car park is on the right just before the road turns left down the hill (⅔ mile).

From Telegraph Hill (see Walk 15): take the B3078 towards Cadnam then the first left (1¼ miles, s.p. Nomansland). The car park is on the right just before the road turns left down the hill (⅔ mile).

From the A36 (Salisbury to Southampton): turn south on to the B3079 at Landford (s.p. Bramshaw – 10 miles from Salisbury, 5 miles from M27 junction 2). Turn right to Nomansland (1½ miles). Go through the village, up the hill, and round the sharp left hander near the top; as you leave the subsequent right hand bend, the car park is on the left (1 mile).

The next three walks follow the top of the escarpment along the northern boundary of the Forest, which also follows the county boundary. To the left is open heathland, to the right are occasional glimpses through trees of the Wiltshire countryside around Whiteparish. The escarpment is of course a watershed, and the streams flow away to your left, south-westwards, to join the Avon. In the pleasant, quiet dell of Crows Nest Bottom (B), however, the two streams wander northward to join the River Blackwater near Landford, which carries their waters to the Test at Totton.

The walk connects the two highest points in the New Forest. At 422 ft, Pipers Wait (A) just shades it by a couple of feet over Telegraph Hill (C). Near the start of the walk is a low flat-topped knoll covered in gorse and young trees which looks artificial – it is; in fact, it is a covered reservoir belonging to the local water company. The top is the highest point you can reach in the Forest without climbing a tree.

WALK 14

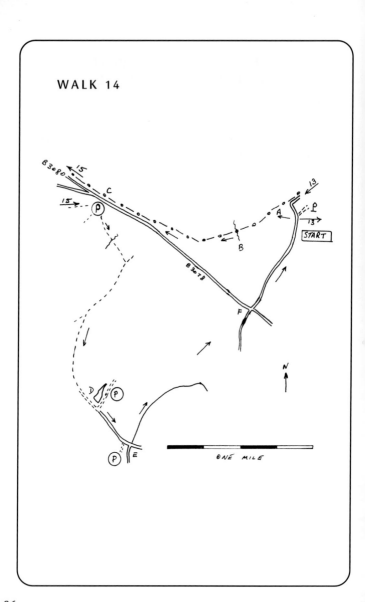

Eyeworth Wood

Telegraph Hill (C) was the site of Bramshaw Telegraph, one of a chain of semaphore stations built by the Admiralty in the early nineteenth century, when there were still fears of French invasion, for communication with Plymouth (there was also a branch to Portsmouth). Letters, numbers, and a few other codes were represented by different settings of an array of shutters. The adjacent stations were near Rownhams and Verwood; men with telescopes watched the transmitting and receiving stations, and when the receiving station repeated a signal, the next letter could be sent. The speed was about six letters a minute, and the daily time signal could be sent from end to end in around a minute.

Eyeworth Pond (D) is obviously man made, having a dam at its foot. It provided a water supply for the Schultze gunpowder

Eyeworth Pond

factory, which operated at Eyeworth from the 1860s to the 1920s, specialising in smokeless powder for sporting guns. The pond is now home to a variety of water birds; the exotic looking ones are mandarin ducks.

As you approach Fritham (E), look out to the right along the track to the car park for a black iron pillar; it is the old post box for the gunpowder factory which saved the postman a half mile round trip. Fritham itself is a small village scattered about the isolated area of pastures around the valleys of two streams forming the headwaters of Dockens Water, which flows southwestwards to reach the Avon valley at Moyles Court (Walks 21 and 22). It has a green, a bus terminus, a chapel and The Royal Oak, which dates back to the late seventeenth century and is the smallest pub in the Forest.

Directions

Cross the road, pass the covered reservoir (A, 300 yds) and turn left by the fence beyond it. *Walk 13 joins here.* Follow the fence down to Crows Nest Bottom (B), keeping left to avoid wet ground on the way down, then bearing right to cross the two streams at the bottom.

Don't worry if the squelchy stream on the opposite slope keeps you left for a while, just follow the fence until you see the sign for the road junction at Telegraph Hill (C, 1¼ miles). *For Walk 15 go straight on.* Otherwise cross the road to the car park. *Walk 15 rejoins here.*

From the back of the car park bear left on a grassy path which drops down the side of a valley. Ford a small stream in the bottom then as you reach trees turn right at the junction (½ mile). This good path is easy to follow to Eyeworth Pond (D, 1 mile). Go straight ahead on the road to Fritham (E, ¼ mile).

A few yards before The Royal Oak turn left on a track labelled 'Farms Only'. There's a fence among trees on the right; when it starts to curve away right, keep going straight on – you'll soon see the signposts at the crossroads ahead (F, 1¼ miles). Go straight over the crossroads and return to Pipers Wait car park just before the left-hand bend (¾ mile). *To return to Walk 13 turn right.*

Near by

Just nudging the 125 metre (410 ft) contour, **Longcross Pond** (1¼ miles) must be the highest stretch of open water in the New Forest, although Janesmoor Pond pushes it pretty close; you may have glimpsed the nearby triangulation pillar as you walked up from Fritham. Although quite small, the pond has a few mallard and its own little island. It is about 5 minutes walk from the car park – turn left along the road, turn right at a low gate (50 yds), follow the track to a defunct car park, whence tall walkers will see the pond; those of lesser stature should bear right. In cold weather wrap up well – it is an exposed place.

• Turn left on the road, then left at the crossroads on to the B3078 (F, ¾ mile, s.p. Cadnam). Take the first right (½ mile, s.p. Fritham). Turn left into the car park (50 yds, SU 251150).

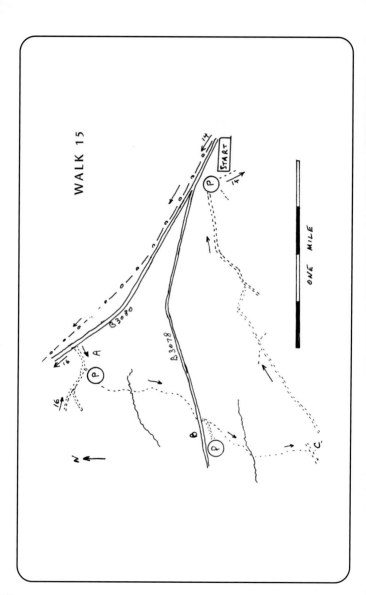

WALK 15

START

ONE MILE

N

B3080
16
A
16
B3078
B
P
C

WALK 15: TELEGRAPH HILL
TO TURF HILL

DISTANCE 4¼ miles (1 mile).

PARKING Telegraph Hill car park (SU 227167) at the junction of the B3078 and B3080.

From Salisbury: take the A338 towards Ringwood and turn left at Downton on to the B3080 for 5½ miles.

From Ringwood: take the A338 towards Salisbury and turn right at Fordingbridge on to the B3078 for 5½ miles.

From Cadnam (M27 junction 1): take the B3079 (s.p. Fordingbridge) then take the left fork at Brook (1 mile) on to the B3078 for 3¼ miles.

The car park is a few yards towards Cadnam from the road junction. It is popular and small; on a nice day, come early. If it is full, take the B3080 (s.p. Downton) to Turf Hill car park (A, 1 mile) and start the walk from there by doing the return leg first.

As with the previous walk, the outward leg follows the road along the high ground of the northern boundary; there is a wide verge, so you don't have to walk right beside the traffic. There are views westwards towards the hills above Cranborne about 10 miles away, and occasional glimpses between the trees northwards into Wiltshire, although recent growth has limited the view in this direction. After ⅔ mile you come to a triangulation pillar on the right – at 407 ft – set back in its own little private recess in the fence. Here the fence and the road diverge slightly; if you follow the fence you will find another of those quiet unfrequented little dells, although wet ground will limit your explorations.

The return crosses Deadman Bottom, climbs Deadman Hill (B) and drops down to Black Gutter Bottom. What splendidly named places for skullduggery! There are streams to cross in both valleys; if it has been wet they can be awkward and Granny may need some help to get across. If it is a cold day, wrap up well. There is no shelter from the wind as it whistles across the plateau.

Near Telegraph Hill

Directions

Cross the road and turn left (*Walk 14 joins here*); take the right fork and follow the road to Turf Hill car park (A, 1 mile). *For **Walk 16** keep going along the road.* Otherwise turn left through the car park (***Walk 16 returns here***).

Keep right of the small pond among gorse about 50 yds behind the car park and go straight ahead on an initially grassy path which curves left in front of trees down to Deadman Bottom. Cross the stream and follow the path up to the road on Deadman Hill (B, 1 mile).

Cross into the access track for Black Gutter car park (at my last visit this car park was closed); where the track turns right, go straight on along the path which slants down the valley side, follow it across the stream in Black Gutter Bottom and up the other side, where it skirts the right hand edge of heather, to a flat area of grass and gravel

which would make a nice big cricket field – a relict of wartime activity to do with a bombing range (C, ½ mile).

Turn left on the track which leaves this area at the far left-hand corner. This will take you back to the car park (1½ miles), *where you can rejoin* **Walk 14**.

Near by

If your journey home is westwards, a visit to **Cadman's Pool** (4 miles) will provide an excuse for a scenic drive across the northern Forest over Ocknell Plain and down through Linwood. The pool is named after its creator Arthur Cadman, who was Deputy Surveyor in the 1960s. It has two islands and small colony of geese. Behind the pond is Anses Wood, a beautiful area of mature woodland, the sort of place where it is easy to imagine Robin Hood and his chums hanging out; your explorations will probably find a path down to the stream of Dockens Water, but be careful not to lose your sense of direction or you'll be late home for tea.

If your journey is to the east, this drive is recommended with Walk 22. If you want to have a shorter expedition and save Cadman's Pool until then, stop off at **Janesmoor Pond**, which is on the left after 2½ miles of the route below. The pond is at about the same altitude as Longcross Pond (see Walk 14), is surrounded by broad areas of firm, level lawn, has plenty of parking and is a popular picnic spot.

• Turn right out of the car park. Turn right at the crossroads (1¼ miles, s.p. Fritham) and right again at the T-junction (½ mile). Take the third right (1 mile – just after Janesmoor Pond at SU 247135). Pass Cadman's Pool car park on the right (1¼ miles, SU 229122), turn right at the T-junction (1¼ miles) and follow the single-track road to Moyles Court (4 miles – see Walk 21). From here you will probably want to take the second right which leads to the A338 (1 mile) near Ringwood.

WALK 16: TURF HILL
TO HALE PURLIEU

DISTANCE 5¼ miles (2¾ miles).

PARKING Turf Hill car park (SU 212177).

From Telegraph Hill (see Walk 15): take the B3080 (s.p. Downton)
and turn left into the car park (1 mile).

From the A338 (Salisbury to Ringwood): turn eastwards on to the
B3080 at Downton; cross the cattle grid (4 miles) and turn right into
the car park (½ mile).

This walk completes the section of high bleak land along the
northern edge of the Forest and turns the corner to the gentler
country of the western boundary as it follows the Avon valley;
you also say goodbye to the county boundary. Psychologically
you are at the halfway point, although not quite in terms of
mileage. The area of heathland you walk on here is Hale Purlieu;
it is one of the commons brought within the perambulation in
1964. The corner is turned at Hatchet Green (B) on the edge of the
high ground (360 ft) above the Avon valley; it is a picturesque
place with thatched cottages, village hall, school and wide green
complete with cricket pitch and is the most northerly point on
these walks.

Rather than follow the boundary along the road from here,
the walk makes an excursion just outside the Forest. The first
landmark after Hatchet Green is Hale Farm (C) where the weath-
erboarded barns stand on mushroom-shaped stones; these are
'staddle stones', the traditional method of keeping out rats. The
route then passes the end of Queen Street – an unusual name for
a short, quiet lane. The track down from this point can be very
muddy, especially at the bottom; try to do this walk in a dry
spell.

Deadman Bottom

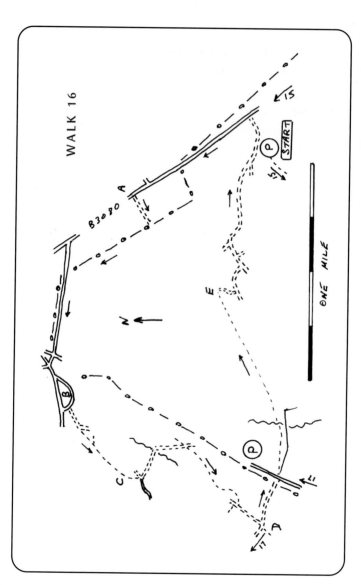

WALK 16

B3080

A

B

C

E

START

P

P

N

ONE MILE

After a bridleway through Stricklands Plantation (to D), a byway brings you back across the boundary where a good path connects with a forest road which returns directly to the car park up on the heath.

Directions

Turn left along the road (*Walk 15 joins here*), cross the cattle grid, then turn left into the track just beyond the telephone box (A, ½ mile). Go through the gate at the end, turn right and follow the fence, then the road (Tethering Drove) to the crossroads (1 mile).

Go straight over the crossroads and take the next turn left to the village green (B). Walk along the left side of the green, and go straight on at the far end through the gate between thatched and tiled cottages on to the bridleway (¼ mile). Keep to the fence on the right, pass through Hale Farm (C), and go diagonally across the field to the gate which leads to the lane at the end of Queen Street (½ mile).

Hatchet Green

Turn left down the muddy track to the valley bottom and up the other side to a signposted crossing halfway up (¼ mile). Turn right and follow the bridleway until it drops down to a junction with a track (½ mile). Turn left.

At the next junction (D, 250 yds) turn right to join **Walk 17**. Otherwise turn left up the hill to the road (¼ mile). Go straight across (**Walk 17** *rejoins here*), follow the path down to the valley bottom (¼ mile), and cross the stream. Climb beside the wood to an electricity pylon (E, ¾ mile – note that forestry operations in progress at my last visit may mean changes on this stretch). Follow the wires for 50 yds and turn right on to a track. Turn left at the T-junction with the forest road (200 yds) and left again at the next one (200 yds), which leads directly to the car park (½ mile) *where you can resume* **Walk 15**.

Near by

It takes some time fully to explore **Downton** (4¼ miles), a lengthy Wiltshire village which straddles the various streams of the River Avon. Two clusters of habitation are joined by a broad main street attractively lined by buildings of various ages and styles. The eastern end has the Norman church and Downton Moot, a land-scape garden of historic origins which runs down to the river – look for a sign to 'The Moot' on the main road a short way up the hill. By the bridge in the main street is a footpath (s.p. Charlton All Saints) which leads to a riverside meadow. There are pubs at either end of the village and one in the middle.

• From Turf Hill car park, turn left on the B3080 and follow it to Downton (4¼ miles). Apart from a few spaces in front of the Co-op (SU 176215), parking is at the roadside.

WALK 17: HALE PURLIEU TO GODSHILL WOOD

DISTANCE 4½ miles (2½ miles); combined with Walk 18 the total distance is 6 miles.

PARKING Hale Purlieu car park (SU 189177) is a mile south of Hatchet Green. The sign is the National Trust symbol, not the usual Forestry Commission type, but don't be confused by another National Trust sign only ¼ mile from Hatchet Green.

From Telegraph Hill (see Walk 15): take the B3080 (s.p. Downton). Take the first left (2 miles, Tethering Drove, s.p. Hale) then first left again (½ mile, s.p. Woodgreen Common). The car park is on the left (1 mile).

From the A338 (Salisbury to Ringwood): turn east on to the B3080 at Downton. When the main road turns left just after The Woodfalls Inn (2¾ miles), go straight on. At the cattle grid (¼ mile) take the left fork and go straight over the crossroads (100 yds). The car park is on the left (1 mile).

In contrast to the wilderness of high heathland on the northern edge of the Forest, the journey southwards starts beside the fertile pastures of the Avon valley, where the boundary follows the river for a short way. The river too is a contrast to the bogs and little streams of the heathland, being the first significant stretch of water since the Beaulieu River at the start of the journey. The route follows the Avon Valley Path for a mile or so of its 34-mile journey from Salisbury to Christchurch.

From the edge of the heath at Hale Purlieu, the walk drops down between fields to Woodgreen Common (B), which has good grass for the ponies and a cricket field; one of the pleasures of village cricket is spending an afternoon standing at long leg in a pretty place like this. Woodgreen has a pub (The Horse and Groom, C), a post office and, oddly but not uniquely, a gated bus shelter. The large gabled brick building seen across the valley from time to time is Breamore House; it is Elizabethan, dating from 1583, although largely rebuilt

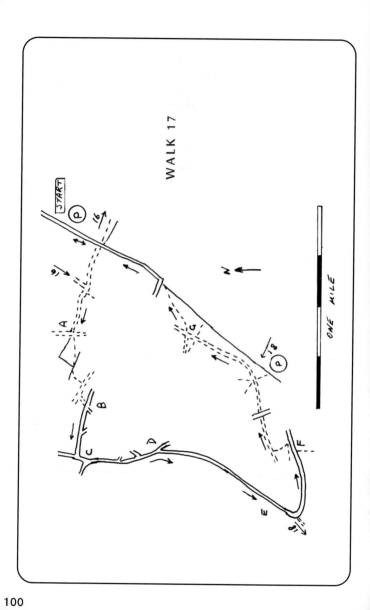

WALK 17

START

ONE MILE

after a fire in the 1850s, and is open to the public.

The road along Castle Hill (D to E) has a lovely view of the Avon Valley – the trees are kept clear in a couple of places to reveal it – and glimpses of the river below. The eponymous 'castle' is an Iron Age hill fort (E); when the road begins to drop down the hill, bear right among trees and stay near the top of the slope to explore its banks and ditches, described on the map as 'ring and bailey'.

The return leg climbs beside a secluded valley (E to F), where the scattered houses, far from seeming an intrusion into the rural environment, add a cosy domesticity to the scene; this 'sleepy valley' is a contrast to your previous encounter with it at Deadman Bottom on Walk 15. A mile through woodland inclosures brings you back beside the middle part of the valley, here called Millersford Bottom.

Directions

Turn left along the road. At the Woodgreen sign (300 yds) turn right over the cattle grid into the unsurfaced lane and pass the bridleway on the right (¼ mile, *Walk 16 joins here*).

Preparing for the match

The Avon and Breamore Mill from Castle Hill

Turn left at the T-junction (A, ¼ mile) then immediately right over the stile (s.p. Footpath). Go diagonally across the first field, along the right hand side of the second, and through a wooded valley. Turn right on an unsurfaced road and follow it round to the left to the road at Woodgreen Common (B, ½ mile).

Turn right, then left at the bottom and pass The Horse and Groom (C). Take the left fork (s.p. Godshill), follow it up the hill, and turn right opposite the cemetery into Castle Hill (D, ¾ mile).

Follow the road along the clifftop (D to E) and down to the bottom of the hill (¾ mile). *For **Walk 18** fork right on the track then turn right at the junction and cross the cattle grid (50 yds).* Otherwise follow the road round the long left hand bend and up the valley side.

As the road climbs out of the valley, note the footpath to the right between 'Godshill Wood Cottage' and 'Highfield' for Walk 18 (F, ⅓ mile). Enter Godshill Wood through the gate on the left (80 yds), take the broad path ahead (not the one going left), turn right on the track (150 yds) and follow it across the road (¼ mile) into Godshill Inclosure.

Pass the point where *Walk 18 rejoins* (¼ mile) to a broad junction with a track from the left (G, ¼ mile); turn right on a path and leave the inclosure through the gate (¼ mile). Turn right on the road which immediately turns left (i.e. go virtually straight on).

At the sign for Hale Purlieu where the land opens out on the right (⅓ mile) *turn right to return to Walk 16*, or go straight on to return to the car park (300 yds).

Near by

Prominent in the view from Castle Hill is **Breamore Mill** (2¼ miles), now a private dwelling. When you've parked the car and walked back over the bridge for a look round there's not much else to do, but it's a pleasant spot to watch the river go by.

• Turn left out of the car park and follow the road to the T-junction in Woodgreen (C, 1½ miles). Turn left and follow the road round to the right of the post office, cross two bridges (½ mile) then immediately turn left and park (SU 162174).

THE IMPORTANCE OF TIMBER

For the first four centuries of their existence, the value of woodlands in the royal forests was seen as the provision of cover for deer and pannage for swine (see 'Ponies and Other Matters'), but by the fifteenth century the production of wood was becoming important. The usual practice was 'coppice with standards', the Crown retaining the rights to the mature oaks (the standards) with the undergrowth of hazel and other trees being periodically harvested (coppiced) by a tenant for fuel. This practice continued until the seventeenth century. In 1483 the first Parliamentary Act provided for enclosure of areas of forest to protect them from browsing deer while regenerating after harvesting. The most effective method of excluding deer was a ditch and bank surmounted by a fence; the remains of many old banks are encountered in the New Forest today.

It is sometimes said that the oak woods of England were cut down to build the Royal Navy; in fact it was gradual clearance for agriculture that destroyed most of the natural woodland. By the seventeenth century, such as remained was coming under pressure from the production of charcoal for iron smelting, although there was not much of this in the New Forest, and it was becoming increasingly difficult to acquire the timber needed for shipbuilding – the construction of a warship required a thousand oaks or more. The shipwrights especially valued timbers with bends which could be exploited in the fabrication of angles in the ship's structure, and these are more common in oaks grown on poor soils such as those of the New Forest. Another important characteristic of the timber required was that it should be found near the coast, because such was the state of the roads that overland transport of freight was very expensive.

The forest system was still geared towards protection of the deer, despite the Crown's lack of interest – James II was the last monarch to hunt in the New Forest – and it was exploited by the local people for their own purposes. The stock of trees suitable for shipbuilding was in decline, and an act of 1698 provided for the enclosure of

6,000 acres in the New Forest for the production of timber, with powers for further enclosures as the original areas matured. This represented a major threat to the area available for grazing, and from time to time during the next 150 years further enclosure was authorised, much to the consternation of the people who depended on the Forest for their living. It was during this period that most of the other royal forests were disafforested.

Matters came to a head with the Parliamentary Act of 1851. This specified that the deer should be removed from the New Forest; they had become a significant nuisance, particularly to surrounding landowners, to whom the Crown had to pay compensation for damage done. For giving up the rights to the deer (that is, being relieved of the liability), the Crown was granted compensation in the form of authority to enclose a further 10,000 acres for forestry. The winter heyning and fence month, whose purpose was to protect the welfare of the deer, were enforced anew, and a register of commoners' rights was to be drawn up. The purpose of the Act is thought to have been to prepare the way for disafforestation, and to limit the amount of compensation to be paid for loss of commoner's rights.

This 'Deer Removal Act' caused an outcry from commoners and local landowners, and from others who appreciated the landscape of the Forest as it was — the coming of the railway in 1847 had increased the number of tourists visiting the area. The proposals were finally abandoned in the 1877 Act, sometimes called the 'Commoner's Charter', which limited the Crown's powers of enclosure, reconstituted the Verderers' Court to protect the interests of the Commoners and recognised the value of the old plantations, today known as the 'Ancient and Ornamental Woodlands'. It also recognised the New Forest as a place of natural beauty with value to the wider community as a place of rest and recreation. It was this Act which laid the foundations for the preservation of the New Forest as we know it today.

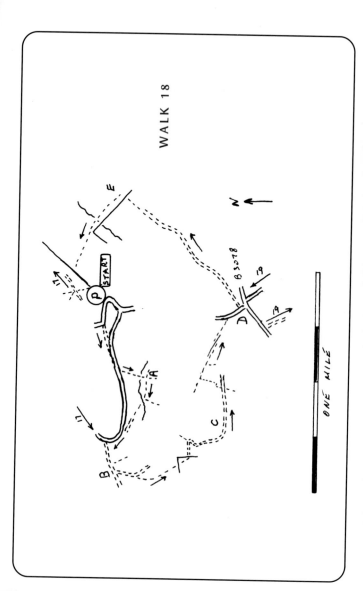

WALK 18

ONE MILE

WALK 18: GODSHILL WOOD TO GODSHILL

DISTANCE 3½ miles (1½ miles).

PARKING Godshill Wood car park (SU 177161).

From the north: turn left off the A338 (Salisbury to Fordingbridge) just south of Breamore (s.p. Woodgreen). On entering Woodgreen (1¾ miles) turn right. After a left hand bend (1 mile), pass Godshill car park, then at a right hand bend (200 yds) turn left into Godshill Wood car park.

From other directions: turn north off the B3078 in Godshill beside The Fighting Cocks (1¾ miles from the A338 at Fordingbridge, 3¾ miles from Telegraph Hill). Pass a left turn (s.p. Woodgreen) then when the road turns sharp left at the top of the hill (¾ mile) go straight on into the car park.

As with Walk 17, you start on the edge of the heath, drop down to the Avon valley, and climb up again through woodland. Much of the walk is just outside the boundary, returning to it at Godshill (D) by the conveniently situated Fighting Cocks. Although the next few walks follow the valley, you get your last glimpse of the river itself – walk a few yards past the turn at (B).

To the left as you walk along the brow of the hanging woods above the valley is Frankenbury (C), another Iron Age hill fort well sited for defence at the top of a steep hill. You need to clamber up left from the path to see the low bank and shallow ditch; the easiest spot is shortly before the path climbs to the same height as the bank. There is little for the layman's eye to appreciate beyond the satisfaction of having found it at all, although the whole thing encloses an area of about 12 acres.

Once again you cross the stream (after E) which has come down from Deadman Bottom (Walks 15 and 17); if the weather has been wet, you'll be pleased to hear that this time you get a footbridge.

Bluebell time near Folds Farm

Directions

From the car park, turn right along the road; when it turns away to the right, go straight ahead on the track, then on the road which joins from the left (¼ mile). Turn left on the footpath between 'Godshill Wood Cottage' and 'Highfield' (100 yds). Cross the unsurfaced lane, go down to the valley bottom, and cross the footbridge (A, 300 yds). Turn right on the path a few yards beyond; bear right to recross the stream at the next footbridge (200 yds).

Go straight on when the path becomes a track, and stay near the fence on the left; turn left through the gate with a cattle grid (¼ mile). *Walk 17 joins here.* Take the second path on the left, on the brow just beyond the farm (B, 200 yds). Turn right on the foot-

path shortly after the fence turns away (200 yds – if you like bluebells, this is the spot for you), cross the stile into the field (300 yds) and bear left to another stile to leave it again (100 yds).

Take the track ahead up the hill, follow it round the bends and then along the top of the slope (C) to the entrance to the caravan site (½ mile, at the start of the tarmac). Cross the stile on the left, follow the path along the right hand edge of the field, and exit at the next stile (200 yds).

Turn right on the path and follow it to the road (straight on at a junction, keep left in the field, cross the stiles over a double fence, keep right in the next field – ¼ mile). Turn right to Godshill Village Hall (D, 150 yds). *For Walk 19 go ahead to the main road and turn right.* Otherwise turn left on bridleway (*Walk 19 rejoins here*) to the open heath (E, ¾ mile). Turn left to the valley bottom, cross the footbridge, follow the path to the top of the valley side and turn left to the car park (½ mile). *To resume Walk 17, enter the inclosure through the gate in the near corner of the car park, follow the path, and turn right on the track (150 yds).*

Near by

As the name implies, **Fordingbridge** (2¾ miles) was important as a river crossing, although commercial activity was originally centred a short way to the south-west near the church; in Domesday the name was *Forde*, the place where later the bridge was built. The

Near Godshill

bridge is medieval, widened in the nineteenth century (look under one of the arches). The 'Near by' expedition for Walk 19 suggests a walk around the town, so for today be content with a short stroll in Fordingbridge Park, the sports field by the river which also has a memorial garden, a children's play area, seats to watch the water from and a good view of the bridge. The George Inn is just across the river.

• Go straight on from the car park to the B3078 at Godshill (D, ¾ mile) and turn right. Pass under the A338 (1¾ miles), take the first left (50 yds) and turn left into the car park (50 yds, pay-and-display, SU 151141). The entrance to the park is a few yards back towards the road.

WALK 19: GODSHILL TO STUCKTON

DISTANCE 5¼ miles (2½ miles).

PARKING Godshill Cricket Pitch car park (SU 182151) on the B3078 (Fordingbridge to Telegraph Hill).

From Fordingbridge: cross the cattle grid (1¾ miles from the A338) and turn right into the car park (⅓ mile).

From Telegraph Hill (see Walk 15): turn left into the car park (3⅓ miles).

Those who seek out rural peace and solitude, who want for a while to leave behind the human race, its noise, and its manufactures, seldom speak highly of ice cream vans such as the one usually found at the car park for this walk. But on a hot summer weekend, what is the attraction of pulling on boots and plodding through fields, wading streams, and struggling across rough heathland, compared with the simple pleasure of sitting by the car, ice cream in hand, watching a village cricket match, saving one's energy for the ten-minute stroll to the pub when stumps are drawn? It's a close run thing. Walkers who doggedly make the effort, and have the further resolve to ignore The Fighting Cocks in Godshill, will be rewarded by the company of Ditchend Brook for the best part of a mile. Anyone who even then regrets the decision can console himself in The Forester's Arms in Frogham (E) on the return leg before having his doubts finally dispelled by the view from the car park at Abbots Well (F) of the sweeping valley of Latchmore Brook on its journey from Telegraph Hill to the Avon at Harbridge. Is this the nicest view in the New Forest? Add it to your list of candidates.

Godshill is a small village scattered either side of the road from Fordingbridge to Cadnam. The Fighting Cocks is so named because there was once a cockpit here; it was just inside the Forest boundary and therefore beyond the local parish jurisdiction.

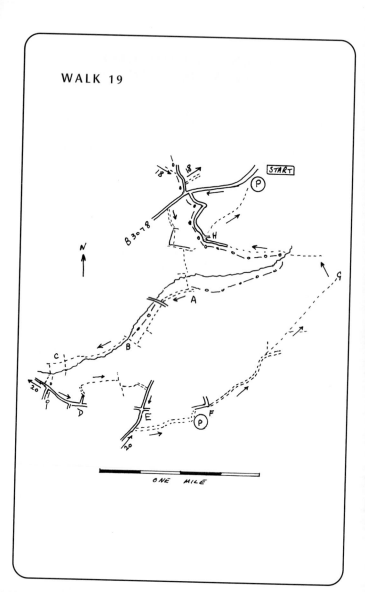

WALK 19

START

N

B3078

ONE MILE

112

The outward leg features a good number of stiles, and the return climbs up on to Hampton Ridge before dropping down to splash across the gravel bed of Ditchend Brook, which was called Black Gutter the last time you got your feet wet in it (Walk 15). If it's all getting a bit much by the time you're climbing up the valley side, just think of that ice cream waiting at the top.

Directions

Turn left along the road, pass the pub (⅓ mile, **Walk 18** *joins here*), and turn left down Well Lane beside the post box (200 yds). Turn right in the field at the bottom (200 yds), cross the stile and turn left, then turn right on a path along the back of a riding school (200 yds).

Just after a right turn, cross the footbridge on the left and follow the path to the open heath below Blissford Hill (A, ¼ mile). Turn right on the track, cross the road to the footpath ahead, keep

Godshill

The Abbot's Well

straight on towards Stuckton at the signpost, and cross the foot-bridge (B, ½ mile).

Turn right, cross another bridge, turn left by the brook and follow the waymarked path (watch out for the point where there is a gate ahead; the stile is about 50 yds to your right). Go straight on at the junction with three stiles (C), take the next left, go over the footbridge, cross the stile on the left and follow the path to the road (²⁄₃ mile). *For Walk 20 turn right.* Otherwise turn left.

Turn left up the lane just beyond the post box (D, ¼ mile). Follow it round to the left, cross the stile at the end (200 yds) and follow the path along the top of the wood. Turn right at the next stile (¼ mile) then take the first left (100 yds). Turn right on to the track at the end, then right again on the road (¼ mile).

Go straight over the crossroads in Frogham (E) then turn left on the track behind the houses (¼ mile, *Walk 20 rejoins here*). Bear right to the car park at Abbots Well (F, ¼ mile).

Return to the road and turn right (the Abbots Well is a spring at the roadside on the right; the open basin is for animals, the covered one for people). Where the road turns left, go straight on (100 yds, s.p. cycle route to Fritham) and follow the track up on to Hampton Ridge. As you come to the brow of the hill (½ mile) bear left on a path to a complicated junction close by; bear right, pass the triangulation pillar (100 yds) and go down the hill to the trees of Pitts Wood (G, ⅔ mile).

Go straight into the wood, turn left at the junction (200 yds) and exit through a pair of gateposts (200 yds – the gate and fence are long gone). Aim to the right of trees ahead, and find a way across the stream (⅓ mile). Follow the path up the hill; after it becomes a surfaced road look out for a branch on the right to Harthill House (H, ½ mile). *To return to **Walk 18**, go straight on, turn left on the main road, take the first right, then right again on the bridleway opposite the Village Hall.* Otherwise, turn right on the path (i.e. not back to Harthill House – if you miss this turn, just turn right when you get the main road) and follow it back to the car park (½ mile).

Near by

For a short exploration of **Fordingbridge** (2½ miles – see also Walk 18), cross the bridge. To the right is a statue by Ivor Roberts Jones of the artist Augustus John (b. 1878), who lived locally from 1927 until his death in 1961; at the mini-roundabout turn left up the High Street. Just past the small Victorian Town Hall, take the left fork as far as St Mary's Church; of Saxon foundation, the present building is predominantly thirteenth-century. Come back towards the town, take the first left (West Street), turn right at the end and return to the High Street. Back at the mini-roundabout go straight on to explore the small area you've missed, which includes the museum and the information centre, then return across the bridge to the car park. The walk can be done in half an hour, but as you will encounter four pubs, a medieval church and sundry other establishments, expect it to take longer.

• Turn left out of the car park on to the B3078. Go under the A338 (2 miles), take the first left (50 yds) and turn left into the car park (50 yds, pay-and-display, SU 151141).

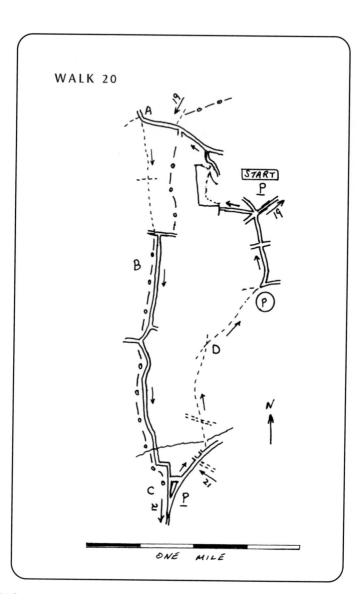

WALK 20

START
P

A

B

C

D

P

19

21

N

ONE MILE

116

WALK 20: STUCKTON TO SOUTH GORLEY

DISTANCE 3¾ miles (2 miles).

PARKING On the verge in Hyde (SU 168125).

From Telegraph Hill (see Walk 15): take the B3078 towards Fordingbridge. Pass The Fighting Cocks in Godshill (3¾ miles) and take the next left (¾ mile – where the main road turns right – s.p. Blissford). Take the right fork into Blissford Hill (¾ mile, s.p. Frogham). Go straight over the crossroads in Frogham (½ mile) and park on the right opposite the school (⅓ mile).

From the A338 (Fordingbridge to Ringwood): turn east into Hern Lane at the crossroads near Bickton (s.p. Hyde – 1 mile from the B3078 at Fordingbridge, 4½ miles from the A31 at Ringwood). Park on the left opposite the school (1 mile).

Starting like Walk 19 at a cricket field, the walk first passes the Church of the Holy Ascension, a comfortable-looking brick building of 1855 on the brow of the hill, hiding modestly within a skirt of trees. You may just glimpse its bellcote as you walk in the valley below. The boundary here follows a road but, as ever, these quiet country lanes around the edges of the Forest are a pleasure to walk along, with verges to keep the feet off tarmac, and in this case opening out to form the village greens of North Gorley (B) and South Gorley (C). There are two pubs, both on the outward leg – The Three Lions at Stuckton (just round the bend from A) and The Royal Oak at North Gorley.

On the outward leg, walking on level ground between green pastures, the open heaths of the Forest could be miles away, but in fact the open commons start above the woods which clad the western slope of Gorley Hill. At a bend in the road shortly after it fords Huckles Brook, the valley permits a glimpse of the brown heather clothes of Dorridge Hill; the upper part of this valley is Latchmore Bottom, seen from Abbots Well on Walk 19.

The return leg climbs Gorley Hill and follows the edge of the

Top: Hyde church
Above: North Gorley

common with contrasting views on either side. To the left is the Avon valley, with Fordingbridge nestling comfortably by the river, and to the right is the Forest hinterland with Frogham and Hampton Ridge (Walk 19) almost ahead. Gorley Common (D) is a plateau of green grass and gorse, and is firm and dry underfoot; the high ground seen to the right is Ibsley Common, which you will cross on the return leg of Walk 21.

South Gorley (C) was the home of Heywood Sumner. Born in 1853 at Alresford, grandson of the Bishop of Winchester, he was educated at Eton and Oxford, then read Law at Lincoln's Inn. He worked however as an artist, and was a leading member of the Arts and Crafts Movement. His wife's poor health took him to Bournemouth, from where he explored the surrounding country-side by bicycle and eventually built a house at Cuckoo Hill in South Gorley, where he lived from 1904 until his death in 1940. He was a keen and much-respected amateur archaeologist, and investigated ancient remains in and around the New Forest and Cranborne Chase; he became the acknowledged expert of his day in all things to do with the New Forest. He wrote the story of his first few years there in *Cuckoo Hill: The Book of Gorley*. It was handwritten and illustrated with watercolour paintings, and pub-lished only in limited edition at the time, but was republished in 1987 for a wider audience; it provides a fascinating account of the life of the village, as well as descriptions of the Forest and Cranborne Chase.

Directions

Take the road to Hyde Church (to the right of the phone box). At the lych gate turn right, go left with the fence, then turn right on a path. Stay up the slope and look out for a fence on the right which leads to a path down to the road (⅓ mile, Pentons Hill). Turn left, then left again at the T-junction (Frogham Hill) and pass Hyde Lane on the left. ***Walk 19 joins here.***

Where the road turns right (A, ⅓ mile), turn left on the foot-path which continues beside the gate of a former transport yard. Follow it along the fence to the road (½ mile, Hern Lane). Turn left, then immediately right into Ringwood Road and follow it

through North Gorley (B) to South Gorley (C, 1 mile).

*For **Walk 21** go straight on.* Otherwise turn left and left again (50 yds). Pass Brookside (200 yds, ***Walk 21** rejoins here*) and take the path on the left (100 yds). Cross the field and the footbridge, and follow the path straight up to the top of Gorley Hill (¼ mile).

Keep to the left and stay on the path along the top of the slope, then bear right on a path which comes up beside a house with four skylights (D, ¼ mile); follow it across Gorley Common to the elbow of the road (⅓ mile, Gorley Lynch). Turn left along the road and return to Hyde school (¼ mile).

*To return to **Walk 19** turn right in front of the school then right again just as you reach the houses of Frogham (¼ mile), on to the track which runs along the backs of their gardens.*

Near by

The New Forest has many beautiful places, but **Latchmore Bottom** (1¼ miles) is one of my favourites; it is the view seen from Abbots Well (Walk 19). Leave the car park away from the stream for a few yards then turn left; as you walk upstream beside Latchmore Brook the landscape opens out to an inviting vista. Alternatively, cross the footbridge from the car park and follow the track up to Abbots Well (10 minutes) for another look at the view.

• Turn left down the side of the school (s.p. Ogdens). Ignore a sign to Ogdens North, and at the dusty crossroads (just under 1 mile) turn left (s.p. 'No Through Road'), carry on when the road becomes unsurfaced, and turn left into Ogdens car park (¼ mile, at SU 182124).

South Gorley

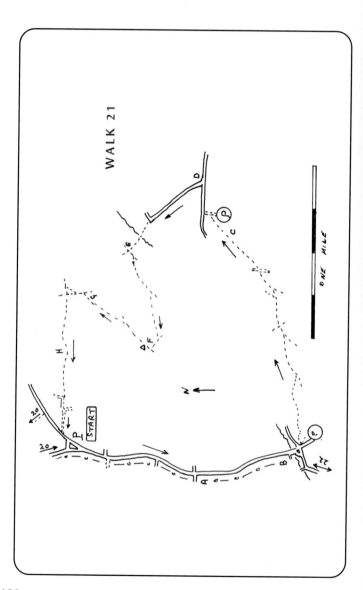

WALK 21

ONE MILE

DISTANCE 5¾ miles (1½ miles).

PARKING South Gorley (SU 162105). No car park here, but space around the village green and its approaches.

From the A338 (Fordingbridge to Ringwood): turn east at a signpost to North Gorley (1¾ miles from the B3078 at Fordingbridge, 3¾ miles from the A31 at Ringwood). Turn right at the T-junction in North Gorley (⅓ mile, s.p. Ringwood) to South Gorley (⅔ mile).

The outward leg follows the road for a mile or so, with the heathery slopes of Ibsley Common to the left. The road is quiet, but expect a few cars on summer weekends. To the right, just after Cross Lanes (A), is a commemorative tablet describing Ibsley Airfield, a World War II fighter base. Much of its extent has been used for gravel extraction, and is now flooded and used by a water company. Beside the lake on the right, birdwatchers will notice a small hide just behind the hedge. The remains of the airfield control tower can be seen to the right a little further on.

Moyles Court (B) was built in the seventeenth century. Now occupied by a school, it was once the home of Alice Lisle, who in 1685 gave shelter to two fugitives from the defeat of the Duke of Monmouth's rebellion at the battle of Sedgemoor. She was betrayed and tried for treason at Winchester by the notorious Judge Jeffreys. The jury at first acquitted her, but under sustained pressure from the judge changed their verdict to guilty, whereupon he sentenced her to be burned at the stake. There was a public outcry at such cruelty and the sentence was later commuted to beheading. She was executed at Winchester at the age of seventy, and lies in Ellingham churchyard (see 'Near by' below).

The return leg climbs on to Rockford Common up a steep path beside a sandy slope that would make the bunker of golfers' nightmares. From the top are fine views across the Avon Valley – the outskirts of Ringwood are to the left, ahead is Somerley House near Ellingham, and north-west is Harbridge church; to the north are the electricity pylons at Hale Purlieu, 6 miles away (Walk 16). The flat landscape of the common is the result of gravel extraction.

From the far end of Rockford Common the walk crosses the valley of Dockens Water at The Red Shoot Inn (D) before climbing up to Ibsley Common. Whitefield Plantation (F) on the brow was one of three planted in 1835 by the second Lord Normanton, the landowner of Ibsley Common at the time, to provide landmarks and add variety to his view from Somerley. There is a good view from the nearby triangulation pillar (at 250 ft) across the valley to the Dorset Hills beyond. Fordingbridge is 3 miles north-west, and the hills of Purbeck are about 20 miles south-west.

The landmark for the next section is a low brick edifice (G), which appears to be a wartime gun emplacement, presumably protecting the eastern approaches to Ibsley Airfield. There are also the foundations of a small building and another bunker (this one is a shelter, not a golfer's hazard). On the way down from the common, where two valleys confine the path to a narrow ridge for a short way, is a low circular earthwork occupied by a spinney of Scots pine; this is Robin Hood's Clump (H), another of Lord Normanton's landmarks, replanted in 1931.

Directions

Walk 20 joins here. Walk south down the road (s.p. Ringwood) past Cross Lanes (A) to Moyles Court (B) and go over the stream to the crossroads (1 ⅓ miles). *For **Walk 22** turn right.* Otherwise cross the road and turn sharp left up the steep sandy path (***Walk 22** rejoins here*) to the top of the hill (200 yds).

There are too many paths on Rockford Common to give all the turns and junctions – basically, just stay above the valley on the left. The route is easier to follow on the ground than to describe, but here goes: Take the left hand path above the valley side. It joins a good

The Avon valley from Rockford Common

Appleslade

path which has been running parallel a short way to the right. Follow this along the top of the bank and go ahead on the path which joins from the other side of the sunken area (old gravel workings; across the valley from here is Whitefield Plantation at F). When you see trees ahead (C, Appleslade Inclosure) cross a track and aim to pass left of them. Follow the path down beside the plantation to the road, passing Appleslade car park (1¾ miles).

Turn right on the road, then turn left at The Red Shoot Inn (D, 200 yds). Follow the lane to a right turn (⅓ mile), but go straight ahead on the footpath, and cross the footbridge (200 yds). Follow the path ahead to a crossing (E, 200 yds).

Turn left, then take a right fork to trees on the skyline ahead (F, ½ mile). Walk to the other end of the plantation and when you see the trig point (200 yds) turn right. Bear left on a path towards a low brick building (G, ¼ mile) then turn left at the next junction (100 yds). Pass the head of a valley and turn left (100 yds).

Follow this path past Robin Hood's Clump (H, ¼ mile), continue beside a fence which comes from the right and go down to the road (½ mile). *To return to **Walk 20** turn right.* Otherwise turn left to the green at South Gorley (100 yds).

Robin Hood's clump

Near by

If you're not fed up with churches by now, go to **Ellingham** (2½ miles). The small, secluded, well-cared-for country church dates from the twelfth century. Its charm comes, however, not from any particular feature – although the Elizabethan rood screen makes a significant contribution – but from the atmosphere and overall effect. The comfort of the pews is enhanced by a noteworthy series of embroideries. In the churchyard, the tomb of Alice Lisle (see above) is on the right as you approach the door.

• From South Gorley, head south (s.p. Ringwood). Turn right at the crossroads (A, ¾ mile), turn left on the A338 (¾ mile, s.p. Ringwood), take the first right (¾ mile, s.p. Ellingham Church) and park at the end of the road (¼ mile, SU 144083).

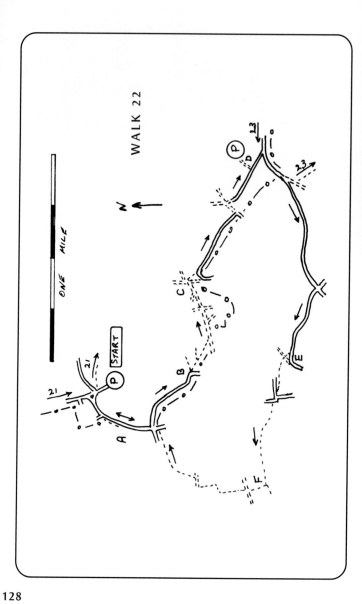

WALK 22

WALK 22: MOYLES COURT TO LINFORD

DISTANCE 5 miles (2 miles).

PARKING At Moyles Court (SU 163084) there is a car park, plus more space at the roadside.

From the A338 (Fordingbridge to Ringwood): turn east at Ellingham Cross (s.p. Moyles Court – 4 miles from the B3078 at Fordingbridge, 1¾ miles from the A31 at Ringwood). Just after a right hand bend, turn left (¾ mile, s.p. Mockbeggar). At the T-junction (200 yds) turn right, go over the crossroads and up the hill (s.p. No Through Road) to the car park (200 yds).

Moyles Court is a popular spot, with space to park, grass to picnic and play on, the stream of Dockens Water, which has flowed down from Fritham (Walk 14), for the children to paddle in, and an ice cream van. It attracts crowds of people on a sunny weekend, but they stay near their cars and are soon left behind. There is a venerable oak at the crossroads, once considered to be the finest in the Forest, although now showing signs of age and the attentions of tree surgeons. A few yards down the road towards Rockford is another ancient specimen which gamely hangs on, although now looking rather geriatric.

The boundary here mostly follows leafy lanes with a scattering of the cottages to which they give access; these are not however the two-roomed cob-and-thatch roses-round-the-door variety but large, comfortable, and, to judge by the cars parked in their drives, expensive family homes. At the far end is another popular picnic spot, Linford Bottom.

The walk reverses the usual anti-clockwise pattern and instead of returning by way of the forest heaths uses footpaths in the Avon valley, which wend their way among the gravel pits. So much of the water in the New Forest is mixed in with the ground you're walking on, in the form of mud and bog, that it is a relief to walk beside some that stays in the ponds where it properly belongs, leaving the paths dry and easy underfoot. Gravel is still being worked here, and other pits are used by a water company; there is sailing at the Spinnaker Club on Blashford Lake.

The Alice Lisle Inn is at Rockford near the beginning and end of the walk (A); it occupies the buildings of what was the village school until the 1960s.

Directions

From the car park, return to the crossroads and turn left (*Walk 21 joins here*). Follow the road round to the left, pass the Alice Lisle Inn (A) and take the first left (⅓ mile, opposite Ivy Lane).

After turning left by a small open-fronted barn, the road turns sharp right (B, ⅓ mile)

At Moyles Court

where two gates invite you to go straight on; take the right-hand gate and follow the path up the hill taking the right fork near the brow to follow the fence. At the end of the fence, climb out of the dip and turn left on the unsurfaced road (300 yds).

Follow this down to a crossing at the valley bottom by Mount Farm (C, ¼ mile). Bear right on the footpath then turn left along the road (100 yds). At the top of the hill turn left on the short unsurfaced stretch then turn right down the hill and pass the entrance to Linford Bottom car park (D, ¾ mile, *Walk 23 starts here*). Go ahead to the road junction and turn right (150 yds, *Walk 23 rejoins here*).

Turn right at the crossroads into Cowpitts Lane (¾ mile, s.p.

North Poulner). Just before a long left bend near the bottom of the hill (E, ⅓ mile) turn right on the signposted footpath, cross the track from 'Waterditch', and hop over the stile. Cross the next stile where the fence on the right comes close to the stream, turn left along a narrow field and leave it by the stile near the right corner almost straight ahead (300 yds). Cross the footbridge.

Turn left on the road then when it turns away right (50 yds) go straight ahead on the footpath. Immediately after the second lake, turn right by an electricity pole (F, ½ mile) and follow the Avon Valley Path waymarks (the symbol is a little bridge) as follows: turn right on an unmade road, turn left on a footpath, turn right on the bridleway at the entrance to the sailing club, turn left by a gate, and turn left on the road. Pass the Alice Lisle Inn and continue to the crossroads at Moyles Court (1 mile). *To rejoin **Walk 21**, bear right and climb the steep sandy path.*

Near by

If your journey home is towards the east, take the scenic route through Linwood and across Ocknell Plain. If you have already visited Cadman's Pool (5¼ miles, see Walk 15), stop off at one of

Cowpitts Lane

the other car parks along the way, for example at **High Corner** (2¾ miles) with its views to the west; the car park is about 200 yds along the track signposted to the High Corner Inn, a surprisingly substantial establishment ⅓ mile further on. If you prefer to visit a woodland inclosure, use the car park at **Broomy Walk** (2½ miles) or **Milkham** (3 miles).

Those heading home westwards will have done this drive after Walk 15, and will no doubt have already spotted somewhere along the route which they want to see again.

• Leave the Moyles Court crossroads heading east (with the prominent oak on your left – s.p. Linwood), passing The Red Shoot Inn, Broomy Walk car park (2½ miles, SU 197100), the turn for the High Corner (¼ mile, SU 199101), and Milkham car park (¼ mile, SU 202102). Take the first left (1 mile, s.p. Stoney Cross), pass Cadman's Pool on the left (1¼ miles, SU 229122), and turn left at the T-junction (1¼ miles). After passing Janesmoor Pond (¼ mile, see Walk 15), this road brings you to the B3078 (1¼ miles) about half way between Brook and Telegraph Hill.

THE MODERN FOREST

Since the 1877 Act, the intention of subsequent legislation has been to preserve the value of the Forest as a special place of benefit to all, and to reconcile the many interests, often conflicting, which affect it. In 1923 the Forestry Commission was given responsibility for management of the New Forest; this created a conflict of interest between commercial forestry and preservation but in 1928 the chairman stated that the amenity value was the main priority. Today, in addition to commercial forestry, they are responsible, in consultation with the Verderers, for management of such matters as drainage, footbridges, deer control, camping, parking and clearance of scrub.

During both World Wars, the New Forest was used for training and exercises and as a holding area, notably of aircraft, men, and equipment for the Normandy landings in 1944. In World War II, the

Ponies drinking at Long Pond

Forest was, as one resident put it, 'one big army camp'; there were airfields at Beaulieu Heath, Holmsley, Fritham, Ibsley and Stoney Cross. Timber production contributed to the war effort, and some land was ploughed for crops. After the war, compensation was paid for damage done, and grazing restored by reseeding.

The 1949 Act reconstituted the Verderers Court on a more representative basis, and the register of Commoners' rights was reorganised as a series of maps – 'The Atlas' – of the land to which rights attach. There was provision for a further 5,000 acres of inclosure, subject to the Verderers' permission; of this allocation, 2,000 acres was actually planted – these inclosures being recognisable by the broad surrounding strip of reseeded grass which acts as a fire break and provides grazing. Those in the south-east of the Forest (Walks 3 to 5) were located so as to provide a visual screen to the industrial areas on the western shore of Southampton Water. The act also authorised fencing of the A31, which was done in 1964 and involved the construction of underpasses, known as 'creeps', to allow the free passage of commoners' animals, such as the one at Picket Post on Walk 23.

The first major change in the boundaries of the New Forest for seven hundred years came with the 1964 Act. There were several surviving commons to the north and north-west of the Forest, for example Cadnam and Rockford Commons, which were adjacent to the Forest and not fenced off from it. The ponies grazing on them were free to wander on to the Forest proper, a custom known as 'vicinage'; they were not subject to the Forest bylaws, the health or breeding controls, nor to the payment of the annual grazing fee. The 1964 Act brought these commons within the perambulation; an area to the south of Brockenhurst was disafforested, but the net result was an increase in the total area. It is this boundary which is followed by the walks in the book. The Act also authorised the fencing of the new perambulation and the installation of cattle grids in the roads entering the Forest to prevent the problem of ponies straying when gates were left open. Other measures autho-rised the fencing of the A35, permitted the Forestry Commission to establish camp sites, and obliged it and the Verderers duly to con-sider conservation of flora and fauna.

In 1970 the fencing was authorised of the remaining main road, the A337. In the following year, the New Forest was designated as a Site of Special Scientific Interest (SSSI), and in the Ancient and Ornamental Woodlands the Forestry Commission was obliged to give priority to conservation over timber production. The biggest changes for the visitor were that cars were constrained to the roads by the use of shallow ditches and short posts, known as 'dragon's teeth', and camping, caravanning, and some other activ-ities were restricted to specific areas.

In the 1980s, the local authority proposed to build a bypass to relieve the traffic problems in Lyndhurst. The Verderers opposed this on the grounds of the loss of grazing land, and the issue was pursued to the House of Lords who decided in their favour. This was an important legal victory, confirming the authority of the Verderers in such matters.

On 1 March 2005, the New Forest became a National Park. Some feel that this imposes an unnecessary level of bureaucracy on a system which already works well enough, and there is concern that while there is no intention to overrule the authority of the Verderers, should conflict arise with the park authority they may not prevail. On the other hand, the National Park includes the wider 'Heritage Area' of surrounding countryside, relieving development pressure on the Forest itself and its immediate fringes, and National Park status should result in improved funding mechanisms.

Timber awaiting collection in Perrywood Ivy Inclosure

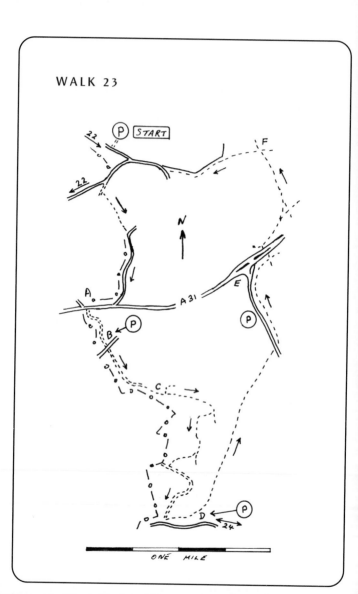

WALK 23

22

22

START

P

N

F

A

A 31

E

P

P

B

P

C

D

P

24

ONE MILE

WALK 23: LINFORD
TO VALES MOOR

DISTANCE 5½ miles (2½ miles).

PARKING Linford Bottom car park (SU 071181).

From the A338 (Fordingbridge to Ringwood): a few yards south of a
bus shelter turn east into Salisbury Road (5¼ miles from the B3078
at Fordingbridge, ⅓ mile from the A31 at Ringwood). The road
immediately turns left and becomes Northfield Road. At the T-
junction turn right (¾ mile, Gorley Road) then first left (100 yds,
Butlers Lane). At the T-junction turn left (200 yds, Linford Road),
then first left (200 yds, s.p. Poulner). Turn left at the signs for the
car park (1 mile) then turn right into the car park itself (150 yds).

The outward leg presents the most hazardous activity on your walk
around the Forest where the boundary crosses the A31. The traffic
is heavy and very fast; do be careful. The crossing represents a psy-
chological milestone in leaving the northern part of the Forest.

Just across the A31 is Hightown Common, now in the care of
the National Trust, which was acquired for public access in 1929 by
the Footpaths and Commons Preservation Society. Its founder,
Baron Eversley, is commemorated by a seat at the car park near by
on the left as you come to Hightown Hill (B). You'll have discovered
by now that the New Forest is particularly short of places where
you can have a sit down without getting damp about the nether
regions, so make the most of it.

The return makes use of Smugglers' Road (from D) which rises
to a little over 300 ft near Picket Post (E); it is even, firm and dry
underfoot and offers fine views. To the south is a typical piece of
peaceful Forest scenery, the open heath gently rolling away beside
Burley Hill, dotted with copses, plantations, and solitary trees;
south-west are the outskirts of Bournemouth, and there are broad
views westwards into Dorset.

As its name implies, Smugglers' Road was a route regularly
used by smugglers. Smuggling was a major industry on the south

Top: Linford Bottom
Above: Pony and foal at Linford

coast for about a hundred years from the mid-eighteenth century. Governments placed heavy duties on imports; as these were mostly high-value luxury goods, there was money to be made from smuggling such things as brandy, tobacco, tea, coffee, lace, silk and even, during wartime, spies and refugees. As many as half the local population might be involved with the smugglers in some way; the innkeepers and the well-to-do as customers, while for the poor agricultural worker a small payment for help given would be a welcome, even necessary, supplement to starvation wages. The contraband was bought legally in France and brought across by the shipload. The smugglers' vessels were fast and well armed, and more than a match for the ships of the Revenue, especially as their captains were skillful sailors with detailed knowledge of the local waters. The goods would be landed at night, and a small army of men, some with ponies, some with wagons, some on foot, would be waiting to carry it away to be hidden inland. Many cottages, inns, and even churches had hiding places; in towns like Lymington and Christchurch, buildings were connected by tunnels so the contraband could be moved about surreptitiously, and spirited away quickly if the Revenue men became suspicious. When smugglers were apprehended, they were often treated lightly or acquitted because the magistrates were probably among their customers, while local jurors would have more sympathy for them than for the government. Smuggling declined during the nineteenth century when the faster and more powerful Navy vessels became available for policing the coasts, and later as customs duties were reduced.

As a large tract of wild and lawless land, the New Forest was ideal territory for the smugglers to hide their booty and transact their business of sale and onward distribution. Just 6 miles or so from the coast, Burley (Walk 24) was a major centre for their activities, with The Queen's Head as one of their meeting places. A well-known local character was Lovey Warne, who would stand on Vales Moor wearing a scarlet cloak as a warning when the Revenue men were about.

Picket Post (E) was at the important junction of the toll road to Poole with the road to Burley, Bucklers Hard and Lymington. The name derives from a picket (i.e. post) which marked the spot, but it may have acquired a second meaning from a picket of soldiers stationed at a strategic point on the smugglers' route. At one time open air sales of contraband were held near by. There was an inn here for most of the nineteenth century, which around the turn of the century became a tea house whose sign was a large golden kettle; it was demolished in 1969. Picket Post remains a place of refreshment, however, as there is now a roadside service area.

Directions

Walk 22 joins here. From the car park turn left, then turn right at the junction (150 yds). Pass the post box and bear left on the track

Smugglers' Road

(300 yds, s.p. Footpath) then left over the stile (100 yds, s.p. Footpath). Following the brook, cross two bridges then bear left to leave the field at the cattle grid (¼ mile). Go straight ahead up the road.

At the A31 (⅓ mile) turn right as far as the bus stop (A, 250 yds) where a gap in the crash barriers allows you to cross the road. Go straight over the cattle grid on to a track and, ignoring footpath signs, follow it round to the left and across Hightown Common to the road (B, ¼ mile, Hightown Hill). Cross to the track opposite, follow it down past Foulford Farm, and cross the footbridge at the bottom (C, ⅓ mile).

Ignore the path on the left and go straight up the hill on a path

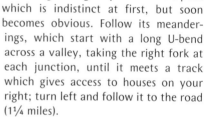

which is indistinct at first, but soon becomes obvious. Follow its meanderings, which start with a long U-bend across a valley, taking the right fork at each junction, until it meets a track which gives access to houses on your right; turn left and follow it to the road (1¼ miles).

Turn left on the road then immediately take a path which bears left and climbs the hill ahead. (*Walk 24 starts and ends at the car park below – D, ¼ mile*). Follow it as it curves left and becomes a broad firm path (Smugglers' Road) rising northwards along the ridge.

Cross the road (1 mile) and turn left beside it. Keep right of the fence which starts at the cattle grid (E), follow the path near by, then turn left through the underpass (½ mile). Turn right at the crossing shortly after you emerge and follow this path, ignoring a right fork as it curves left to a clump, predominantly of holly (F, ½ mile). Turn left down the hill, keep to the left by the gate and follow the fence, then the road back to Linford Bottom (¾ mile). *To return to* **Walk 22** *follow the road round to the left.*

Near by

One conjectural derivation of the name of the busy market town of **Ringwood** (2½ miles) suggests that, like Fordingbridge, it was important as a river crossing. Its market charter was granted in 1226; nowadays the market is held on Wednesday mornings. Many of the shops occupy the ground floors of older buildings, and do so less obtrusively than in many towns, helping to preserve its character. There are some delightful old tile roofs as well (always look up when you walk along a High Street – what is above is usually much better than what is below), and the modern building is in most cases respectful of its surroundings. The interior of the large nineteenth-century church is impressive, and has an unusual marble pulpit, alabaster font, and much stained glass.

For a short tour, leave the car park with the Furlong shopping centre on your right, and keep going to Market Place. Turn right to the end, where you'll find the church, and continue into West Street as far as the river, passing the house where the Duke of Monmouth was held after his unsuccessful rebellion in 1685. In the opposite direction, Market Place leads to Christchurch Road, where numbers 44 and 86 are of sufficient distinction to be mentioned in Pevsner's *Guide to the Buildings of England*. Real ale enthusiasts will cross Castleman Way, on the route of the former railway line (see Walk 25), and continue the pilgrimage as far as number 138, the Ringwood Brewery, before returning to explore the rest of the town centre.

• From Linford Bottom car park turn left, then right at the T-junction (150 yds). Turn right again at the next T-junction (1 mile), left at the next (¼ mile), and right at the one by The White Hart (¼ mile). Cross the mini-roundabout and the bridge over the A31, and go straight on at the roundabout (½ mile; SU 148055) to the town centre car parks (one of which appears to offer Short Stay Toilets).

Dedicated boundary hoggers will either turn right along the road to the boundary or go straight across and follow the ridge southwards; they are unlikely to find a way of crossing Bagnum Bog or Strodgemoor Bottom without wet feet or a twisted ankle. Those content that others have suffered that they might not will eschew such feats of derring do and turn left along the road as directed below.

The route southwards is about a mile within the boundary, below the slope of Burley Hill from Castle Hill (E) to Burley Beacon. At the southern end is Long Pond (B); although near the road, it feels remote, reflecting the inhospitality of much of the boggy terrain between here and the boundary. Ponies come here to drink, you may see the heron who gives his name to Crane's Moor, and in summer you may see dragonflies and the water lilies in flower.

As you take the return leg north-east from Burbush Hill (C), a gap in the higher ground to the south-east gives an unexpected glimpse of the Isle of Wight, about 20 miles away. A little further

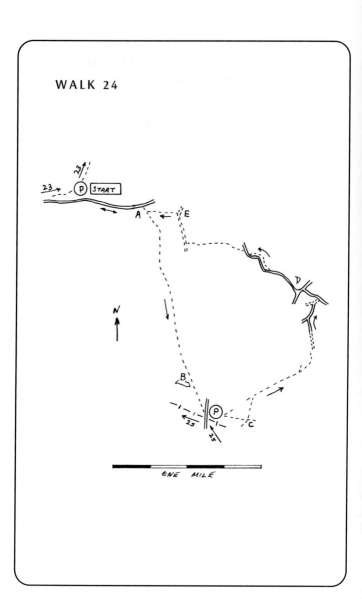

WALK 24

ONE MILE

on, the top of Sway Tower (see Walk 28) pops into view 5 miles away.

The name of Burley (D) is Saxon, from *burgh* ('fortified place'), presumed to be the hill fort on Castle Hill, and *leah* ('meadow' or 'clearing'). It is not named in Domesday, but is possibly one of the entries mentioned under Ringwood. In the fifteenth century, Sir Morris Barkley reputedly killed a dragon here; a wolf has been suggested as a possible explanation – they became extinct in this country not long after. The village has a large car park and many visitors, and sits astride a road that gets busy at the weekends. It offers teas and ice creams, antiques and knick-knacks, groceries and souvenirs, as well as The Burley Inn and The Queens Head. This latter was once the haunt of smugglers (see Walk 23); a notice inside refers to a tradition that it has stood here at least since 1633, and a glass panel set into an internal wall reveals the laths of what may have been one of the original walls. The Burley Manor Hotel dates from the nineteenth century, and stands on the site of the old manor house.

On Castle Hill (E) is an ancient hill fort. The remains are easy to find – indeed you can follow the bank in a complete circle if you don't mind dodging the occasional holly. Don't be too preoccupied with archaeology, though, to miss the fine view south-west across Cranes Moor towards Bournemouth, with Purbeck beyond, about 20 miles away.

Long Pond

Directions

Walk 23 joins here. From the car park, turn left along the road; shortly after crossing a stream turn right at a car barrier on to a path (A, ⅓ mile). Take the right fork (50 yds) and follow the broad path, always taking the bigger looking path at junctions. Don't worry too much about navigation, because most branches join up again; pass beyond the slope of Burley Hill on your left to Long Pond (B) and go ahead to the road (1⅓ miles); turn right for a few yards to Burbush Hill car park. *Walk 25 starts and ends here.*

Go through the car park, bear slightly left across the grass, cut through the narrow belt of trees, follow the path to the top of the hill (C, ¼ mile) and turn left. Stay on this path, keeping the trees to your left, to Goats Pen Cottage, then take the track beside it. Two right turns will bring you to the road opposite the school (1 mile). Turn left.

Go down the hill past The Queen's Head and into the village (D, 250 yds). Stay on the major road, and as you leave the village take the path on the right opposite Clough Lane (¼ mile, s.p. Burley Street). When it rejoins the road (300 yds) take the path on the left (50 yds, s.p. Footpath) through the right-hand of three gates.

Turn right on the track (½ mile). At its highest point (E, ¼ mile) turn left across the grass and drop down the hill to the road (A). Turn left to return to Smugglers' Road car park (¾ mile). *To rejoin Walk 23, climb the hill behind the car park and turn right on the path at the top.*

Near by

Having just walked through the centre of Burley, you may be interested to take a short drive round the periphery of the village to get an idea of its extent and nature. For a stopping off point, try **Mill Lawn** (3 miles), which is an extensive area of good firm grass with a nice stream to follow. Alternatively, in summer when the heather is in bloom go to **Clay Hill** (5½ miles); the old road to Lymington is open as far as the car park. Walking further on through the heather, you'll reach the A35 at Wilverley Post in about a quarter of an hour, passing a surprisingly well maintained milestone on the way.

Near Burley Manor

• Turn left out of Smugglers' Road car park then turn right at the junction (¾ mile) to Burley Street. Turn left into Forest Road (¼ mile), turn left again at the T-junction (1 mile), then take the first right (¼ mile, Mill Lane). Pass Mill Lawn car park on the left (¾ mile, SU 223034) then turn left at the T-junction (200 yds) and keep left into Bisterne Close. Turn left at the next T-junction (1½ miles) then sharp left at the five-way junction (200 yds) to Clay Hill car park (½ mile, SU 232024).

On returning to this junction from Clay Hill, turn sharp left on Station Road for the A35, go straight on through Burley for the A31, or turn right for The White Buck Inn (200 yds).

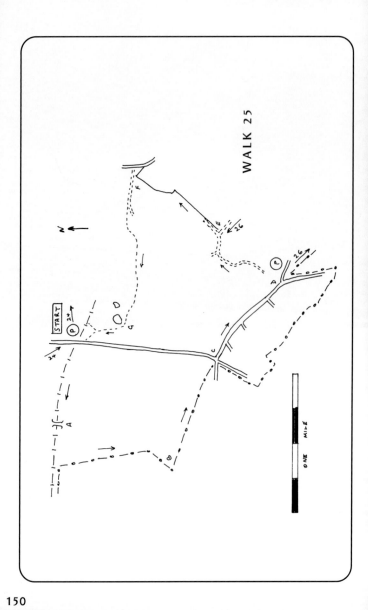

WALK 25

START

ONE MILE

WALK 25: BURBUSH HILL
TO HOLMSLEY

DISTANCE 6½ miles (3½ miles).

PARKING Burbush Hill car park (SU 202019).

From Picket Post (see Walk 24): follow signs for Burley. In the village (2½ miles) where the main road bends left, turn right in front of the War Memorial (s.p. Bransgore). The car park is on the left (1 mile).

From the A35 (Lyndhurst to Christchurch): turn off at signs to Burley (6½ miles south of Lyndhurst, 3¾ miles north of The Cat and Fiddle – from either direction take the slip road on the left then turn left at the T-junction). As you enter Burley (2¼ miles) follow the road round to the left by The Queen's Head, but go straight on (s.p. Bransgore) where it turns away right at the War Memorial. The car park is on the left (1 mile).

Most of the walk is well away from roads, and the first half especially quiet, around Dur Hill Inclosure, where relatively elevated ground (rising to about 200 ft) gives pleasant views; ups and downs mean, as ever, muddy ground in the dips. At Avon Clump (B) you come to the end of the southward journey along the western boundary, and start heading east. It's a fair way to go yet, but at least you can hold the map the right way up; full steam ahead for Bucklers Hard!

The first mile or so follows the waterlogged cutting of the former Southampton and Dorchester Railway (SDR). The London and South Western Railway (LSWR) opened to Southampton in 1840, giving the city an advantage over rival ports. When Charles Castleman, a Wimborne solicitor, promoted the SDR he was supported by the ports of Poole and Weymouth, and by landowners wanting access to new markets for their agricultural produce. The line ran via Totton, Ringwood, Wimborne and Wareham, and opened in 1847; in the New Forest there were stations at Lyndhurst Road (now Ashurst), Beaulieu Road,

Brockenhurst, and Christchurch Road (at Holmsley). Access to Christchurch was improved by the Ringwood, Christchurch and Bournemouth Railway, which opened in 1862, although it was not extended to Bournemouth until 1870; from West Moors, the Salisbury and Dorset Junction Railway opened in 1866, serving the Avon valley northwards. There was also a branch to Lymington (see Walk 28). The lines were operated by the LSWR in return for a share of the profits, and it had absorbed them all by 1883. During this period, Bournemouth had grown from a village to a sizable town, and in 1888 the LSWR opened a direct route from Brockenhurst via Sway and New Milton to the existing line at Christchurch; this knocked about 8 miles off the journey and is still the main line to Bournemouth and Weymouth. The line south from Ringwood now became an unimportant rural branch and eventually closed in 1935, by which time the LSWR had become part of the Southern Railway. The line west from Brockenhurst, which this walk follows, and the northward branch to Salisbury were closed by British Railways in 1964. In the mid-nineteenth century, the railway enabled more people to visit the New Forest and enjoy its unique nature, making an important contribution to the desire to preserve it.

About half way along the railway cutting a bridge (A) gives access to Brown Loaf on the southern edge of Cranes Moor where the view opens out to reveal Vales Moor ahead (Walk 23) and Burley Hill to the right (Walk 24).

At the further end of the walk, the car park (D) is at the site of the former Holmsley Airfield, which was operational from 1942 to 1946, and was used for a variety of purposes including anti-submarine patrols, bombing missions and support for the D-Day landings.

Directions

Walk 24 joins here. From the car park turn left on the road, cross the bridge over the former railway line, and turn right, following the cutting. After passing a bridge on the right (A), use a

Brown Loaf

broad path a few yards to the left to follow the cutting to the end of the inclosure (1 mile); cotton grass here suggests wet ground in the corner. You are back to the boundary; turn left.

Follow the fence on the switchback path to Avon Clump on Whitefield Hill (B, 1 mile); look back for a view to Vales Moor and Smugglers' Road (Walk 23). Turn left with the fence. At the end of the inclosure, the view half left is of Burbush Hill at the start of the walk.

Follow the fence to the crossroads (C, 1 mile, Cross Ways) and go straight over into Forest Road. Shortly after passing Black Lane on the right, turn left into the access road for Holmsley caravan site (D, ¾ mile). *For **Walk 26** go straight on by the fence on the right.* Otherwise turn left into the car park.

Turn left again to leave it. Turn right at the end of the holly just after a prominent oak, and follow the track to the corner of Holmsley Inclosure (E, ½ mile). Take the left fork (*Walk 26 rejoins here*) and keep the fence on your right as the track becomes indistinct; follow the fence as it detours left around what appears to be a duck zoo (the premises of a wildfowl breeder).

Go ahead to a good gravel track and turn left (F, ¾ mile). When it bends left to an old quarry, go straight on following a broad path along the ridge; on the skyline ahead is Dur Hill Inclosure (A to B). Follow the path down to Whitton Pond (G, 1 mile) and pass it on the left, casting about among gorse for a dry passage. Turn right to Burbush Hill car park (⅓ mile), *where you can return to **Walk 24**.*

Near by

Christchurch Quay (9½ miles) is close to the point where the Avon and the Stour join forces to flow into Christchurch Harbour. On the land between are the castle ruins and the magnificent twelfth-century priory. For a short walk, leave the car park at the far end, turn left through the small park below the priory, and turn left again through the wall near the end. Follow the path beside the mill leat, through the park, and past the castle to Bridge Street (the bridges over the Avon are to the right). Turn left to the end of the High Street, turn left again and enter the priory gate, then bear right and return to the car park. Leaving the same way as before, go straight on by the marina housing to view the riversmeet, or turn right for the old water mill and the riverside of the Stour.

• Turn left out of Burbush Hill car park, take the first left (C, 1 mile), turn left at the T-junction (1½ miles), then turn right on the A35 (½ mile). Turn left in Christchurch (5¾ miles, s.p. Town Centre). Go straight over the mini-roundabout towards the priory gate, follow the road right, take the first left, and go straight on into the Priory car park (⅓ mile, pay-and-display, SZ 159924); if it is full, you'll find more parking further along the road.

Holmsley Ridge

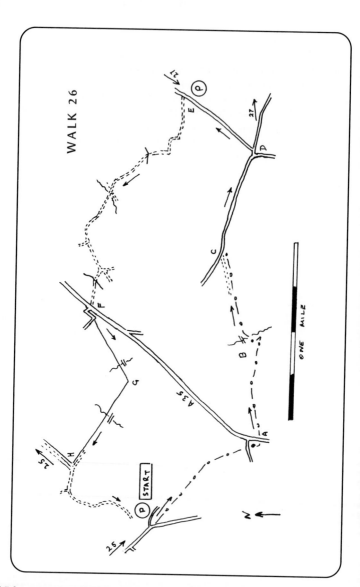

WALK 26

ONE MILE

156

WALK 26: HOLMSLEY TO WOOTTON

DISTANCE 6 miles (2½ miles).

PARKING Holmsley Walk car park (SZ 211993).

From Picket Post (see Walk 24): pass Burbush Hill car park (see Walk 25) then take the first left (1 mile, Forest Road). Turn left into the access road for the caravan site (¾ mile), then left again into the car park.

From the A35 (Lyndhurst to Christchurch): turn west at a sign to Godwinscroft (8 miles south of Lyndhurst, 2 miles north of The Cat and Fiddle). Take the first right (½ mile, Forest Road); turn right into the access road for the caravan site (¾ mile) then left into the car park.

A level walk, after the ups and downs of the previous one, especially the first bit over Plain Heath, and no difficulty in following the boundary; the return is through woodland inclosures for the first time in a while. You cross the A35, last seen in Ashurst (Walk 8), and return to the southern part of the Forest. On the way back, you recross it at Holmsley Toll House (F) – it was originally the toll road to Christchurch.

Beside Holmsley Road (C to D) is a granite horse trough; it is dated 1887 and bears a worn

Heath spotted orchid

157

Pony and foal near Holmsley Toll House

inscription which appears to include the words 'presented to the Corporation of Brighton', but that is all I can make out; see if you can do any better.

Nicely situated at the far end of the walk – half way for circular walkers – is The Rising Sun (D).

Directions

From the car park cross the caravan site access road to the fence, and turn left along it. *Walk 25 joins here.* Go through the gate on the right, turn left on the road, cross the A35 and through the gate opposite (A, ¾ mile).

Go ahead on an indistinct path with occasional wheel marks which keeps trees about 50 yds to your right; continue on a better path which joins from the right and drops down a broad gap between the trees to the bottom of a dip – there is a footbridge to the right (B). Climb the other side of the valley and go ahead to Holmsley Road (C, 1 mile).

Turn right along the road, which soon opens out on the left. Where the main road bends right at The Rising Sun (D, ½ mile) go straight on into Tiptoe Road. *For **Walk 27** keep going straight on.* Otherwise turn immediately left again (s.p. Brockenhurst).

Take note of Broadley car park (⅓ mile) for Walk 27, then turn left beside a large modern house (E, 100 yds) on to a gravel track (*Walk 27 rejoins here*) and follow through the inclosures. Leave by bearing right to a gate when you see it (1¼ miles) and go ahead to the A35 (F, 250 yds). Turn left on the road, immediately right into the side road, follow that round to the left, then when it turns sharp right go straight on past the front of Holmsley Keeper's Cottage and cross the stile (150 yds).

Follow the fence of Holmsley Inclosure on your right, initially keeping left to avoid wet ground. At the bottom of the dip (300 yds) return to the fence to cross the bridge, and follow it uphill beside a screen of sweet chestnuts giving way to pines.

Turn right with the fence at the top (G, 350 yds) and follow it to the next corner (H, ½ mile). *Turn right to return to **Walk 25**,* or turn left to return to the car park (¾ mile).

Near by

Everybody likes a trip to the seaside, and no excuses are offered for suggesting a visit to **Mudeford Quay** (6¾ miles) at the narrow entrance to Christchurch Harbour. You'll find a promenade to stroll on with views of Christchurch Bay, the Needles and, inland across the harbour, Hengistbury Head, Southbourne and Christchurch. There's a café, a fish shop, a pub and lots of boats.

• Turn right out of the car park, then left at the T-junction (100 yds). Turn left at the next T-junction (¾ mile) then turn right on the A35 (½ mile). At the second roundabout turn left (4 miles, s.p. Mudeford) then turn right at the next roundabout (⅓ mile, s.p. Mudeford). Just after a small parade of shops on the right (1 mile), turn left (s.p. Mudeford Quay) to the car park (200 yds, pay-and-display, SZ 184918).

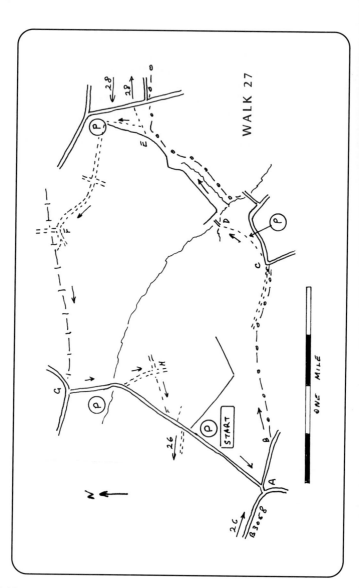

WALK 27

ONE MILE

WALK 27: WOOTTON TO SET THORNS

DISTANCE 4¾ miles (2½ miles).

PARKING Broadley car park (SZ 237989).

From The Rising Sun at Wooton (on the B3058, 1¼ miles east of the A35, 1¼ miles north of the B3055), turn into Tiptoe Road (s.p. Sway) and immediately turn left (s.p. Brockenhurst). The car park is on the right (½ mile).

Starting near The Rising Sun at Wootton (A), the outward section follows the now familiar pattern, with the boundary separating heathland from fields and houses. It drops down from Boundway Hill (C) to a footbridge over Avon Water (D), which makes its way to the Solent at Keyhaven; in wet weather a small tributary in front of the bridge swells to a large puddle which may involve some paddling.

On the return, the route passes through the caravan site in Set Thorns Inclosure (F); the Forestry Commission has placed its caravan sites carefully, and you would not normally see them unless you were to seek them out. The caravans are scattered about a large area of woodland and the site is quiet, presumably because of the nature of those caravanners who seek out such places; this site remains open in winter, when a surprising number of hardy souls can be seen.

There follows a section (F to G) on the trackbed of the former railway, which here is a broad gravel track, in contrast to the swampy cutting near Burbush Hill (see Walk 25). Even at walking pace, there is a feeling reminiscent of railway travel as you walk along a line which remains level against the gentle rise and fall of the terrain.

Winter colours on Boundway Hill

Directions

Turn left along the road to The Rising Sun (A, ⅓ mile) and turn left again on Tiptoe Road. *Walk 26 joins here.* Near the chapel, leave the road by bearing left of the telephone box (B, 300 yds). Follow the fence on the right, then the gravel track beside it, and go straight ahead on the road (C, 1 mile, Boundway). Bear left on a path (50 yds) and follow it as it drops gradually across the slope.

At the bottom cross the footbridge (D, ¼ mile – if wet, the driest route will be found by splashing about among trees on the left). Turn right at the fence ahead, and follow it when it turns

left (100 yards). When the fence curves away left (E, ½ mile) *go straight up the hill and cross the road for **Walk 28***, otherwise turn left on a path a few yards up the slope.

At Set Thorns car park (⅓ mile, ***Walk 28** rejoins here*) enter the inclosure through the gate and follow the track ahead. Go straight on through the caravan site, following the main track around a few bends. Just before the old railway bridge (F, ½ mile) turn left then first right, go through the gate, and turn left along the trackbed of the former railway line. When your way is barred by a bank (¾ mile) escape to the left, go forward to the road junction (G), and turn left (s.p. Wootton).

Recross Avon Water at Wootton Bridge (¼ mile) then enter Broadley Inclosure by a gate on the left (100 yds). Follow the track to the first crossing (H, ¼ mile) and turn right on a grassy ride. When your exit is barred by what used to be a gate (¼ mile) turn left beside the fence to a functional gate (100 yds) and turn left on the road. At a gravel track beside a modern house (100 yds) *turn right to rejoin* **Walk 26** or go straight on to return to the car park (100 yds).

The former railway line at Set Thorns

Near by

Barton on Sea (4½ miles) stands on the cliffs above Christchurch Bay and is a good place for blowing the cobwebs away in winter. There are clifftop walks, views from the Solent to Purbeck, access to the beach and, if that's not enough for you, teas and ice creams too.

• Turn left out of the car park towards The Rising Sun (A, ½ mile), turn right, then immediately left (s.p. B3058 New Milton). Go through New Milton town centre and turn right at the roundabout (2¾ miles, s.p. Barton on Sea). Turn left at the

traffic lights (½ mile, s.p. Barton on Sea), keep left of the memorial (¾ mile) and turn left at the T-junction to the car park (100 yds, pay-and-display, SZ 239930). There is some parking at the road-side, and additional car parks in both directions, that to the west being slightly more convenient.

PONIES AND OTHER MATTERS

No view of the New Forest would be complete without its scattering of ponies. In the unlikely event of none being seen, their existence can in any case be inferred from the landscape; because of their grazing, they have been called 'the architects of the New Forest scenery'. The origin of the breed is unknown, but they have been here at least since the Conquest and possibly much longer. Because of various attempts to improve the breed from the Middle Ages onwards, the nature of their original predecessors is also unknown.

The New Forest pony is a sturdy animal, and in previous centuries many were sold as draught and pack animals, and to collieries. Nowadays its even temperament makes it suitable as a riding pony for both adults and children, and the many unfenced roads in the Forest mean that it is well used to traffic. The breed is hardy enough to live all year on the open forest, but this doesn't mean that they are wild animals in the usual sense; in fact they are all owned by people – the Commoners – and each one carries the owner's brand. Their welfare is monitored by the Agisters, whose numbers vary depending on prevailing circumstances – usually there are about five; each patrols his own area of the Forest and contacts a pony's owner if necessary. In the autumn 'drifts', each covering a few square miles, the ponies are rounded up and some are taken for the sales held five times a year at the sale pens beside Beaulieu Road Station. Those returned to the Forest are mostly mares; stallions have to be approved and registered to maintain the qualities of the breed. They are branded, wormed and fitted with reflective collars in an attempt to reduce road accidents – over a hundred are killed on the roads every year. At the same time, the Agister cuts the pony's tail to his own pattern to signify that the annual grazing fee has been paid, which is why it's called the 'marking fee'.

While you were expecting ponies, you might be surprised the first time you come across a small herd of apparently 'wild' grazing cattle. In former times they were often domestic dairy cattle, but today they are usually beef cattle 'stored' on the Forest between purchase and sale. Ownership is indicated by ear tags (ponies' ears are too sensitive for this practice, which is why they are branded). On your walks no doubt you will eventually encounter donkeys as well. Numbers fluctuate, but typically there are about 3,000 ponies and 2,000 cattle; donkeys are numbered in dozens rather than thousands.

In turning out their animals to graze on the Forest, the Commoners are exercising a statutory right that dates back to the Middle Ages. Their rights attach to a plot of land, rather than belonging to an individual, and the register is a series of maps. As well as the right to *graze ponies and cattle*, there are five others, though not all Commoners have, or exercise, all of them. The right to *graze sheep* on the Forest is rarely exercised. The right of *mast* refers to the practice of pannage, which is to turn pigs out on the Forest; unripe acorns are harmful to ponies and cattle, but harmless to pigs, which are turned out for two months in the autumn to hoover them up. The right to cut turf (peat) for fuel is *turbary*, which is no longer exercised. Nor is the right of *marl*, which was the digging of a limey clay for spreading on the land to improve its fertility; there were once about two dozen marl pits in the Forest. Finally there is the right of *estovers*; originally the gathering of dead wood for fuel, it is now provided by the Forestry Commission, which makes the appropriate quantities available for collection by those who retain the right.

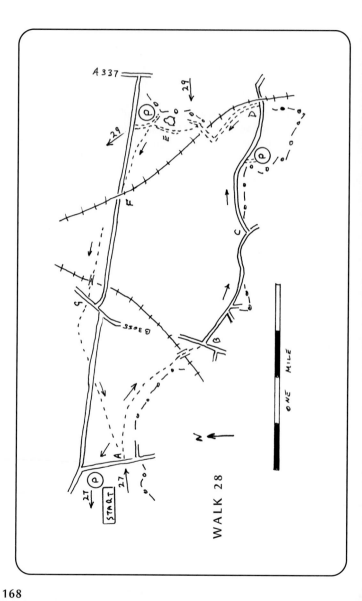

WALK 28

WALK 28: SET THORNS TO SETLEY POND

DISTANCE 5¼ miles (3⅓ miles).

PARKING Set Thorns car Park (SZ 273998).

From Picket Post (see Walk 24): go through Burley (2½ miles), pass under the A35 (2 miles), and proceed from * below.

From Christchurch: turn left off the A35 at a sign to Burley (3¾ miles after The Cat & Fiddle) and turn right at the T-junction (200 yds, s.p. Sway). * Take the second right (1¾ miles, s.p. Sway), then the first right (1¼ miles, s.p. Sway), and turn right into the car park (100 yds)

From the A337 (Brockenhurst to Lymington): turn west at a sign to Burley (1¾ miles from Brockenhurst, 1½ miles from the railway bridge at Lymington). Turn left on the B3055 (1 mile) then immediately right (s.p. Burley). Take the first left (¾ mile, s.p. Sway) and turn right into the car park (100 yds).

First, a warning: there is a lot of gorse on this walk; as it grows, the directions may change – and think twice before doing it in shorts.

After crossing the main railway line (B to G, see Walk 25), the route crosses the branch line to Lymington (D to F). The port was suffering from falling trade because of the silting up of the estuary and competition from Southampton, as well as the decline of the salt works; the Lymington Railway, opened in 1858, was seen as way of restoring prosperity. The London and South Western Railway took it over in 1879, bought the Solent Steam Packet Company, and built a new station at Lymington Pier which ships could use at any state of the tide. Before electrification in the 1960s, the Lymington services were the last duties of the celebrated 'Schools' class locomotives; at the time of writing, this is the last place you can see the old electric 'slam door' trains.

At the far end of the walk is Setley Pond (E) where you may see people sailing radio controlled model yachts, a commendably quiet hobby.

On the return leg there are views of the long chalk ridge of the Isle of Wight which runs west towards The Needles; geologically it forms the southern edge of the Hampshire Basin. Also prominent to the south is Peterson's Tower, a mile beyond Sway. Andrew Peterson was a retired Indian High Court judge who built the tower as his mausoleum, completing it in 1885; he was a spiritualist, and believed that he was guided by Sir Christopher Wren. It was an early use of concrete, and in its day it was, at 218 ft, the world's tallest concrete structure.

The Hare and Hounds is a mile along the outward leg (B), and provides temptation to linger early on.

Broadley Inclosure

Directions

Turn right on the road. At the sign for the cattle grid (A, 300 yds, **Walk 27** *joins here*) turn left on a path across the heath, then take a broad right fork (200 yds). Be guided initially by overhead wires near by on the right. Cross the railway bridge (¾ mile) and bear right to the road at Sway War Memorial (B, 200 yds – The Hare and Hounds is to the right). Cross into Pitmore Lane.

Take the first left (C, ½ mile, Shirley Holms) follow the road to the railway bridge (D, ¾ mile) and turn left on the track in front of it.

Follow the track right at Coxhill Cottages (⅓ mile) and cross the railway bridge. Immediately take a path on the left and

follow it as it curves right and passes left of Setley Pond (E, ⅓ mile). *Walk 29 starts and ends at the car park.*

About 100 yds past the car park take a path on the left, follow it to the railway bridge (F) and go under it (⅓ mile).

The path you really want here has become badly overgrown with gorse and is difficult to find; if you prefer not to walk along the road, try the following: Turn right beside the railway line. Turn left opposite the railway colour light signal (300 yds). Turn left again when the gorse permits (about 300 yds) and aim for Sway Tower. You should find a good path in about 100 yds; turn right and follow it across a footbridge over the (other) railway line (¼ mile).

Take the least prickly option to the road ahead (G), cross it

Setley Pond

and follow the path up the hill and round to the left. At the road (½ mile) the reason why the path is dead straight is revealed by a low sign indicating the position of a gas pipeline. Follow it across the road at an angle, then keep to the right of a covered reservoir (A) to return to the car park (½ mile), *and to resume* **Walk 27**.

Near by

Milford on Sea (7¾ miles) seems to suffer less from motorcar blight than many places and with its shops beside the village green it retains a sort of 1930s charm. The church, 5 minutes walk north from the green, is externally undistinguished because of pebble-dash rendering, but inside it is roomy and inviting, the atmosphere being much helped by a thoughtful lighting scheme. The main body of the church is from the Early

English period with later additions in the Decorated style and some surviving features of the earlier Norman church at the western end.

The beach (½ mile south) is opposite The Needles, 2 miles away, and at the start of the long shingle spit which creates the narrowest point of the Solent – just under a mile – and leads to Hurst Castle which, like Calshot Castle (Walk 2), was built by Henry VIII with stone from Beaulieu Abbey.

At **Keyhaven** (1 mile east) the salt marshes and mud flats provide a habitat for seabirds, waders, and small boats, one of which ferries visitors to Hurst Castle. To walk on the shore in either direction, leave by the far corner of the car park then turn right either on the road or the footpath.

• If you wanted to go to Milford you probably wouldn't start from Set Thorns, but here goes: Turn right out of the car park, go through Sway, and turn right at the crossroads on to the B3055 (1¼ miles, s.p. New Milton). At a sign to Everton and Hordle turn left (1½ miles) then left again (100 yds). At the mini-roundabout (1 mile) turn right then take the second next left (100 yds, Stopples Lane). Turn right at the T-junction (1 mile), cross the A337 at The Royal Oak (¾ mile, Downton Lane) then turn left on the B3058 (½ mile, s.p. Milford on Sea).

In Milford (1¾ miles), turn right down the far side of the green (s.p. Keyhaven) to the crossroads (100 yds) and either turn left for Keyhaven (1 mile, pay-and-display, SZ 306915) or go straight on for the village car park (100 yds, pay-and-display, SZ 291918) and the beach (½ mile, pay-and-display, SZ 292912).

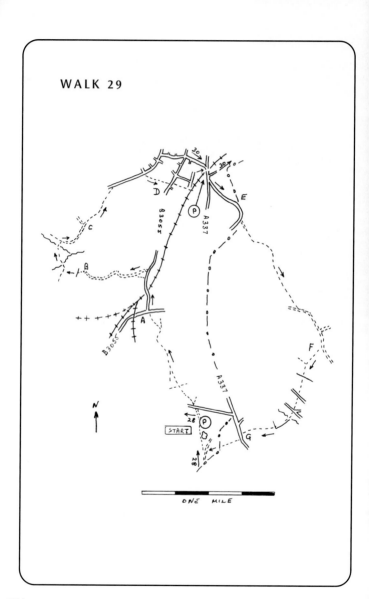

WALK 29

B3055

A337

30

30

D

E

C

B

A

B3055

P

START

P

28

28

A337

F

G

N

ONE MILE

WALK 29: SETLEY POND TO BROCKENHURST

DISTANCE 6½ miles (3½ miles).

PARKING Setley Pond car park (SZ 302992)

From Picket Post (see Walk 24): go through Burley (2½ miles), pass under the A35 (2 miles), then proceed from * below

From Christchurch: turn left off the A35 at signs to Burley (3¾ miles after The Cat & Fiddle) and turn right at the T-junction (s.p. Sway); * take the 2nd right (1¾ miles, s.p. Sway), turn left on the B3055 (2 miles) then immediately right; the car park is on the right (¾ mile).

From the A337 (Brockenhurst to Lymington): turn west at a sign to Burley (1¾ miles from Brockenhurst, 1½ miles from the railway bridge at Lymington). The car park is on the left (¼ mile).

So as not to follow the boundary along a main road, this walk sets off inside it by way of Setley Plain and Brockenhurst Manor golf course, and returns outside the boundary through Roydon Woods. The walk just skirts Brockenhurst, leaving the centre of the village for the return leg of Walk 30, but you may like to know that there are two pubs conveniently situated for half-way refreshment near the level crossing. There is also The Hobler Inn near the end of the walk.

The original railway line (see Walk 25) turned west across the Forest just south of Brockenhurst; looking down from the bridge in Sway Road (just after A) it was about 100 yards beyond the point where the Lymington branch turns away left, but all you'll see today are the trees which have grown across the point of divergence since closure in 1964.

Brockenhurst Manor is the only golf course crossed by these walks (to B). Although conservationists worry that the growing number of golf courses may reduce the range and diversity of available habitats, they are nevertheless pleasant landscapes, like

a modern equivalent of the 'natural' parkland laid out around great houses in the eighteenth century.

The return leg starts up Church Lane (to E), of which John Wise wrote in 1862:

> For a piece of quiet English scenery, nothing can exceed this. A deep lane, its banks a garden of ferns, its hedge matted with honeysuckle, and woven together with bryony, runs, winding along a side space of green, to the latch-gate, guarded by an enormous oak, its limbs now fast decaying, its rough bark grey with the perpetual snow of lichens, and here and there burnished with soft streaks of russet-coloured moss; whilst behind it, in the churchyard, spreads the gloom of a yew, which, from the Conqueror's day, to this hour, has darkened the graves of generations.

The oak is gone, but the yew remains. Wise quoted its circumference as 17 ft; a yew of that size would typically be about 400 years old, so it may not be quite as ancient as he suggested, but today at the least it would be well into its sixth century.

The graveyard (E) contains the graves, with a memorial to them, of about 100 New Zealand soldiers who were among thousands brought to Brockenhurst for hospital treatment in the First World War. A little further up is a separate enclosed plot containing the graves of the Morant family, one time Lords of the Manor of Brockenhurst. A few yards towards the road from the New Zealand memorial is the resting place of Harry 'Brusher' Mills (1838–1905), a local character whose nickname came from his duties brushing the cricket pitch at Balmer Lawn. He was a snake catcher and supplied live snakes to London Zoo to feed the hamadryads (king cobras), which feed on other snakes.

The church itself is the oldest in the New Forest. The doorway and nave are Norman, the chancel thirteenth-century, and the

St Nicholas, Brockenhurst

tower dates from 1761. Wise described the 1832 north aisle as 'a new staring red brick aisle, which surpasses even the usual standard of ugliness in a dissenting chapel', but perhaps with the passage of time we may look on it more kindly today. The stained glass is nineteenth-century, the chancel lancets being particularly enjoyable. The church is open in the afternoons during the summer months; if you arrive at the wrong time, at least see the Norman doorway in the porch.

About a mile of the return leg is through Roydon Woods Nature Reserve, a Site of Special Scientific Interest (SSSI) in the care of the Hampshire Wildlife Trust.

Directions

Walk 28 joins here. Return to the road, turn left for 50 yds, then turn right on to the left-hand of two paths. Follow it across Setley Plain until you see trees and a tiled roof ahead (½ mile). Take the left fork through a belt of gorse; pass right of a cottage to the road (A, 300 yds).

Cross into Sway Road then turn left into the drive of Brockenhurst Manor Golf Club (⅓ mile). Pass immediately to the right of the clubhouse (¼ mile) on to a track across the course. As you approach Blackhamsley House (¼ mile) cross the plank bridge on the right, follow the waymarks around the back of the 14th tee (B) and cross the stile (50 yds). Go straight across the grass, keeping right of a low knoll, and turn right on a sandy path (200 yds).

Ignore a right fork (¼ mile), cross the plank bridge over the stream, and at the top of the slope turn right. When the track turns left (C, ¼ mile), go straight on into a short cul-de-sac, through the gate at the end, and follow the path over various stiles to Burley Road (⅓ mile). Turn right.

Opposite Armstrong Lane (¼ mile) turn right on a path to Sway Road beside a school (D, 300 yds). Turn left on the road, then right on the footpath (50 yards). Turn left at the next road end (200 yds), go through the station car park and over the level crossing (¼ mile).

For **Walk 30** take the first left (50 yds, Mill Lane). Otherwise take the second left (100 yds, Church Lane, s.p. Parish Church,

Walk 30 rejoins here). Pass the church (E, ¼ mile) then take the bridleway on the left (250 yds) into Roydon Woods.

Follow the path, going straight ahead on a bridleway which joins from the right; pass a bridleway on the left then turn right on a path (F, 1¼ miles, s.p. Bridleway). Follow this out of the wood and across two roads and a footbridge; go up the left-hand side of the field and follow the path to the main road by The Hobler Inn (G, 1 mile). Turn left.

Turn right on the footpath down the near side of a white house (50 yds – look back to see the signpost); when you emerge on to the open heath go ahead through gorse, cross the gravel track (¼ mile) and immediately bear right on a path to Setley Pond car park, *and the return to* **Walk 28**.

Near by

The next three 'Near by' suggestions take the popular route across the middle of the Forest from Brockenhurst via Rhinefield (Walk 30) and Bolderwood (Walk 31), starting with **Ober Corner** (4½ miles). The main attraction here is the stream of Ober Water; explorations along the bank downstream will be limited by muddy ground even in summer, but the adjacent track leads to Bolderford Bridge (½ mile – turn left out of the car park), popular with families of small children who like paddling, where the stream joins Highland Water (which later becomes the Lymington River).

• From Setley Pond, turn right out of the car park and turn left on the A337 (¼ mile). Take the first left (½ mile, s.p. Burley) then second right to join the B3055 (A, ½ mile, Sway Road, s.p. Brockenhurst). Take the first left (1 mile, The Rise, s.p. Rhinefield) and turn right at the T-junction (300 yds, s.p. Rhinefield). Turn right (1 mile, s.p. Aldridge Hill), pass the first car park and turn left into Ober Corner car park (¾ mile, SU 285036) just before the road turns away right.

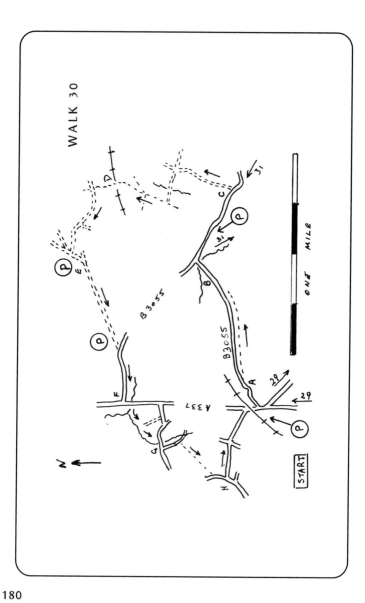

WALK 30

ONE MILE

180

WALK 30: BROCKENHURST TO IVY WOOD

DISTANCE 4½ miles (1 mile). Walk 31 is fairly short; the combined distance is 7½ miles.

PARKING Brockenhurst Station (pay-and-display, SU 302021) at the level crossing on the A337 (Lyndhurst to Lymington).

If you don't want to pay, park at Ivy Wood and start from there (between B and C – see Walk 31 for directions).

Starting from the station, the walk heads along Mill Lane, beside Brockenhurst Park, home until 1958 of the Morant family, some-time lords of the manor, the park being laid out in the late eighteenth century by Edward Morant. After passing North Lodge (A), a rather fanciful building in an ornate French style, the route uses a permissive path just inside the park before returning to Mill Lane, at the far end of which (B) is 'Mill House' at the site of the water-mill which once stood here beside the Lymington River.

After crossing the river, the walk returns by way of woodland enclosures to Balmer Lawn (F), a popular spot where in summer you'll find an ice cream van and a cricket match. During World War II, the Balmer Lawn Hotel was used as a military headquarters during the run up to D-Day.

The remainder of the walk takes a trip around part of Brockenhurst village before returning along the main street, Brookley Road (from H). Although the present village developed after the arrival of the railway in 1847, it is old enough to have been included in the Domesday Book. It is popularly supposed that the name means 'Badger's Wood', but the older spelling of 'Brokenhurst' may indicate a broken (i.e. fragmented) wood, although it is also suggested that it derives from the personal name *Broca*.

North Lodge, Brockenhurst Park

Directions

From the car park cross into Mill Lane (50 yds south of the level crossing). **Walk 29** *joins here.* Just after North Lodge (A, ¼ mile), enter Brockenhurst Park through the small gate on the right, follow the path beside the road to the next gate (½ mile) and return to the road. Pass Mill House (B) on the left, and go ahead to the road junction (¼ mile).

For **Walk 31** *turn right along the river bank.* Otherwise turn right along the road, pass the white railings at the bottom of the dip, and enter a gate on the left into the inclosure (C, ⅓ mile, s.p. Cycleway, **Walk 31** *rejoins here*). Follow the forest road to a

crossroads (⅓ mile) and turn left. Turn right at a T-junction on to a grassy ride (¼ mile) and follow it, ignoring a right fork, as it narrows to a path and crosses a railway bridge (D, ¼ mile). Go ahead through the gate to a gravel forest road (200 yds) and turn left. Turn left again at the junction by Standing Hat car park (E, ⅓ mile), and when you come to the road (½ mile) go straight ahead along it.

By the Balmer Lawn Hotel (F, ¼ mile) turn left on the main road, cross the bridge, then turn right through a gap in the hedge (20 yds – by the lamp post) and down the steps. Go ahead on the path and follow the bank of the stream to the road by the Cloud Hotel (G, ¼ mile). Turn right, then immediately turn left into Butts Lawn. At the end (100 yds, by the ford), turn right on the footpath.

At Burley Road (¼ mile) turn left, pass a private footbridge, turn left over the footbridge at the ford (H, 150 yds, The Watersplash) into Brookley Road, and follow it back to the station (⅓ mile). *To return to **Walk 29**, go over the level crossing and take the second left (100 yds, Church Lane).*

Near by

Rhinefield Ornamental Drive (3¾ miles) is lined with Redwood and Douglas Fir planted in the 1850s, now some of the tallest trees in the Forest. As you will drive this way en route for

Mill Lane

Bolderwood after Walk 31, why not stop at Blackwater car park and explore the area on foot, either following the 'Tall Trees Trail' (1½ miles) or visiting the arboretum across the road?

• From the level crossing bear left along Brookley Road through the village to the Watersplash and turn right (⅓ mile, Rhinefield Road). Blackwater car park is on the right (3½ miles, voluntary pay-and-display, SU 268047).

WALK 31: IVY WOOD
TO HEDGE CORNER

DISTANCE 3½ miles (1¾ miles).

PARKING Ivy Wood car park (SU 045024).

From Lyndhurst: take the A337 towards Brockenhurst. At the Balmer Lawn Hotel turn left (3 miles, s.p. B3055 Beaulieu). Pass Mill Lane on the right (1 mile) then turn right into the car park (200 yds).

From Lymington: take the A337 towards Brockenhurst. Just before the level crossing turn right into Mill Lane (3½ miles after the railway bridge, s.p. B3055 Beaulieu). Turn right at the T-junction (¾ mile) then turn right into the car park (200 yds).

From Beaulieu: take the B3054 (s.p. Lymington). When it turns off for Lymington (1¼ miles) stay on the major road which becomes the B3055; the car park is on the left (3¾ miles).

The walk starts with a short stroll along the bank of the Lymington River before it turns away towards Roydon Woods (Walk 29). The path rises gently out of the valley past the clutch of cottages at Dilton, to Roundhill camp site, another of the discretely placed large quiet caravan sites, which springs to life at Easter. A sweep round the perimeter of the site leads to a path through Perrywood Ironshill Inclosure and back to the river bank.

The water tank which acts as a guide at the far end of the walk (B) has the good manners to be painted green, albeit in a brighter shade than formerly; our modern way of life requires many artifacts, such as radar domes, water towers, caravans and wind turbines, which we accept for the benefits they bring – but why do people always insist on painting them white, when green or brown would be so much less intrusive?

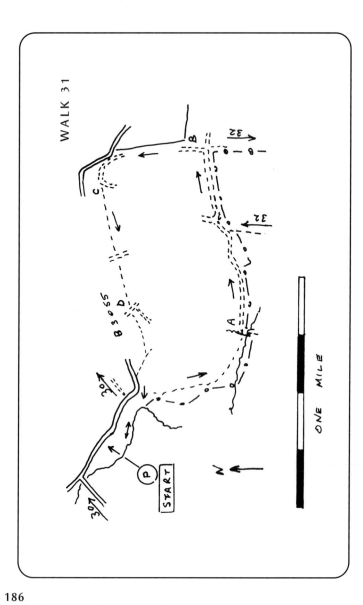

WALK 31

ONE MILE

N

186

Directions

Go down to the riverbank and turn left. *Walk 30 joins here.* When a fence bars the way (¼ mile) turn left and follow it up the slope. Turn right on a broad grassy path at the top (200 yds). When the fence turns away right (½ mile) stay on the path and follow it over a stream to join a gravel track ahead (A, 300 yds).

Follow this as it rises beside the cottages of Dilton, and turns to concrete. *Walk 32 rejoins here.* Take the right fork as it joins the perimeter road of the caravan site (½ mile), and follow it towards a large green water tank high in the trees (B). The earthwork on the left surrounded by a low fence is Pudding Barrow.

At a crossing (100 yds before the water tank), *turn right for Walk 32,* otherwise turn left. Follow the inclosure fence almost to the road (⅓ mile), turn left on a gravel track and left again on an old tarmac one. Go through the gate on the right opposite a

The Lymington River, Ivy Wood

Near Lodge Heath

camper's water tap (C, 250 yds — no fence, just a gate).

Following the broad grassy ride, cross the access road for the caravan site and the next track (D — ignore the grassy track near by on the left), and go straight ahead on a path through the trees to a T-junction (¾ mile); turn right to the bend in the road (300 yds). *To return to **Walk 30**, turn left on the road then enter the gate on the right (50 yds).* Otherwise go down the slope to the river bank (100 yds) and follow it back to the car park (¼ mile).

Near by

The **Bolderwood** car park (8¼ miles) is by the deer sanctuary — there is a viewing platform a few yards down the hill from which deer can often be seen. There is also a selection of short woodland walks. The suggested route to Bolderwood is by way of the popular

IVY WOOD TO HEDGE CORNER

Rhinefield and Bolderwood Ornamental Drives through beautiful woodland in the heart of the Forest. Along the way you may be interested to stop off at the Knightwood Oak, thought to be the oldest tree in the Forest – cross the road from its car park, choose either fork in the path, and return by the other.

• From Ivy Wood car park, turn left along the road then turn left at the T-junction on to the A337 at Balmer Lawn (1 mile). Take the first right (¼ mile, Meerut Road) then turn right at the T-junction (½ mile, s.p. Rhinefield). Go straight across the A35 (4 miles) to the Knightwood Oak car park on the left (300 yds, SU 265064), then continue to the Bolderwood car park on the right (2⅓ mile, voluntary pay-and-display, SU 243086).

Fallow deer at Bolderwood

FLORA AND FAUNA

The New Forest contains large areas of habitats that were once common, but are now rare – lowland heath, pasture woodland and valley bog. It is important particularly because of the unusually wide diversity of species, although these do include a number of uncommon ones – particularly the wild gladiolus, the Dartford warbler, the smooth snake and the sand lizard. I recognised long ago, however, that nothing I ever see turns up in the 'uncommon' section of the reference book. Wild creatures are anyway likely to disappear at the approach of a walker's boots, and the best way to observe wildlife is to pick a likely spot and sit still – not an activity this author is very good at. The valley bogs especially are not suitable places for walkers – a fact discovered the hard way several times during the explorations for this book. All this is not to say that if you keep your eyes open you won't see plenty of things that you'd not see if you stayed at home to wash the car; just don't expect the place to be teeming with exotic species on display like some kind of zoo.

An advantage of walking around the fringes of the Forest is the quantity and variety of flowers in the hedgerows, especially in spring. On the heaths there is plenty of gorse, which is a mass of yellow flower in spring; it provides an important supplement to the ponies' winter diet and, like holly, it is nutritious, if prickly. There is also a dwarf gorse which flowers in summer. Heathland derives its name from heather, which gloriously carpets large areas with purply-pink flowers in July and August.

When it comes to birds, you will hear, and sometimes see, lapwing, curlew, woodpecker, wheatear and stonechat, as well as more familiar species; although you will occasionally see the odd buzzard, there are few birds of prey because the poor soil supports relatively few earthworms on which their prey, such as shrews, would feed.

Before the Deer Removal Act of 1851, there were around 8,000 deer, and they were a major nuisance in the Forest and the lands round about; the Act decimated the population rather than completely eliminating it, and today the Keepers maintain their numbers at about 1,500. You won't see them often because they tend to spend their days in woodland and only come out on to the open heath at dusk, and anyway they are shy creatures which make off when they spot you even when you are some distance away; in woodland you will usually get closer to them than on open ground. In my experience the best strategy when you do see them is quickly to dodge behind a tree – sometimes when you peep out again you will be lucky and find that they haven't gone very far.

The most common are fallow deer, thought to have been introduced by the Normans. They feed in groups, have a black and white rear end and grow to about 3 ft at the shoulder. Their summer coats are chestnut with white spots, and in winter they are dark grey or mulberry, although other colours, including white, do occur.

Roe deer are also common; they feed in ones and twos, have no noticeable tail and are smaller, being about 2 ft at the shoulder. Their coats are red-brown in summer, grey-brown in winter.

You are less likely to see any of the small numbers of muntjac or Japanese sika deer, or of the red deer, the largest native species, which is 4 ft at the shoulder (sika are between fallow and roe, and muntjac are smaller than roe).

When it comes to boys and girls, fallow and roe are bucks and does, whereas red are stags and hinds; for progeny, fallow have fawns, roe have kids and red have calves.

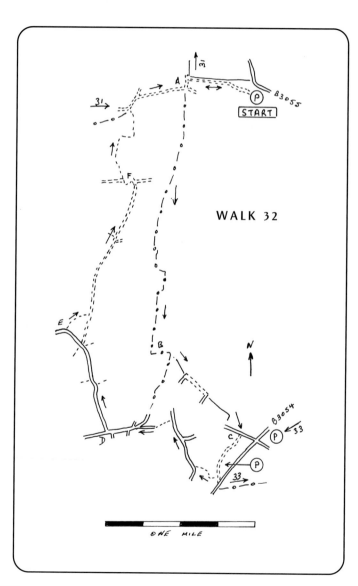

WALK 32

B3055

START

B3054

33

N

ONE MILE

192

The outward leg follows the boundary as usual, with heathland to the left and green pastures to the right. Once again the hills of the Isle of Wight are ahead, about 10 miles away. The return leg uses footpaths and lanes just outside the boundary.

In Bull Hill (C), you pass a Caravan Club 'Certified Location'. Those who are not caravanners may be surprised at the contrast with the large sites passed on previous walks. These small locations are limited to five caravans and short stays, and have minimal facilities; they are often on farms, and are ideal for self-sufficient caravanners who like quiet places. I believe the Camping and Caravanning Club offers something similar.

The parish church of St John the Baptist, Boldre (E) is a picturesque affair set on high ground overlooking the valley of the Lymington River. Its remote location is not untypical of the New Forest, being situated in the middle of a large parish, rather than at a particular village. It celebrated its 900th anniversary in 1987, although few signs of the original Norman church remain, the building, like most old churches, having been much altered over the years; much of the present structure dates from the fourteenth century. The church contains the memorial to H.M.S. *Hood*, which was sunk in battle with the Bismarck off Iceland in 1941 with the loss of over a thousand men. Robert Southey, Poet Laureate from 1813 to 1843, married his second wife here in 1839. The Rev. William Gilpin, vicar from 1771 to 1804, was a well-known travel writer and champion of the 'picturesque'; he used much of the income from his writing for the benefit of his parishioners. Those who enjoy country churchyards will be pleased to hear that this one covers three and a half acres.

The first pub encountered since Brockenhurst is The Fleur de Lys in Pilley near the start of the return leg – go straight on from D for 100 yds (thirsty one-way walkers equipped with a map will find a route to it from B).

Directions

Facing back to the road, take a track on the left (west) through a disused car park and beside the inclosure to a green water tank up in the trees (A, ¼ mile). Turn left on the concrete track and go straight on when it turns away right (100 yds). *Walk 31 joins here.* Follow the path, which is sketchy in places and wet in others, but stays within 100 yds of the fence, until you come to a low bank ahead around an area of pasture with cottages visible beyond (B, 1¾ miles).

Turn left along the bank, go straight on when it turns away right (100 yds) and join another bank on the right (100 yds); this becomes a hedge, and the path becomes a gravel track. When it

The church of St John, Boldre

turns away right to a road (¼ mile) go straight on beside the fence. When this too turns away right (⅓ mile) go up the slope ahead to the brow (50 yds). Turn right and aim to hit the road 50 yds left of the end house (C, 200 yds).

Cross the road into the track opposite and follow it to a footpath on the right (⅓ mile). *For Walk 33 go ahead to the road and cross over (100 yds).* Otherwise (*Walk 33 rejoins here*) cross the stile and the next one (behind the shed on the right), then the footbridge, and follow the path to the road (¼ mile). Turn right.

Go straight on at the next junction (300 yds) then turn left on to the footpath just after the bus stop (250 yds). The path becomes a road; turn left at the junction (¼ mile). Opposite the War Memorial Hall (D, 300 yds) turn right into Church Lane then turn right on the footpath just before the church (E, ⅔ mile).

Keep right in the field, then turn left on the track at Haywards Farm (300 yds). At Dilton Farm (F, 1 mile) follow the path left behind barns then go straight across the track at the other end of the farmyard (100 yds) on to a path beside another barn. Turn right on the concrete track (⅔ mile, *rejoin Walk 31 here*). Take the right fork (150 yds) turn left (¼ mile) to the water tank (100 yds) then turn right to the car park (¼ mile).

Near by
Rans Wood (2 miles) at Furzey Lodge is only a mile from Beaulieu, but like so many of these little places in the Forest, it could be a long way from anywhere. From the car park, the track leads down through an attractive open area of small trees and scrub to Hawkhill Inclosure where it climbs the gentle slope of Moon Hill beside tall, silent pines. Alternatively, go straight on from the end of the road and cross the stream to a path that winds through Stubbs Wood, a beautiful area of mature woodland. If you prefer water to look at, stop off at **Hatchet Pond** (1½ miles), an artificial pond, originally a series of marl pits, by the junction with the Lymington road.

• From Stockley car park turn right on the road. Pass Hatchet Pond car park on the right (1½ miles, voluntary pay-and-display, SU 369017) and turn left (50 yds, Furzey Lane); Rans Wood car park is on the left (½ mile, SU 366025).

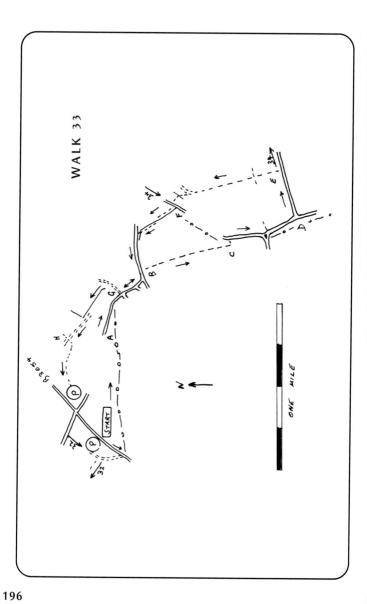

WALK 33

ONE MILE

START

After passing through the small village of Norleywood (A to B), whose name just refers to the northerly location of woodland relative to South Baddesley, you encounter for the first time a signpost (between C and D) to Bucklers Hard, your ultimate destination; only two more walks to go after this one! The walk passes the end of Tanners Lane (D), which provides the only public access to the Solent shore along the boundary; it is suggested as the 'Near by' expedition for Walk 34, but if you prefer to do it on foot you will want to know that the shore is half a mile down the lane.

Because of enclosed land and wet ground near East End (F), the return leg retraces the outward route for a short way through Norleywood (B to G), giving you time to ponder on the reasons for the various house names – perhaps like me you will need to look some of them up when you get home. The last stretch (from G) is a woodland walk through Norley Inclosure.

The East End Arms (between C and F) can be visited on either leg of the walk.

Directions

Return to the road and turn right. Turn left at the cattle grid (200 yds, *Walk 32 joins here*) and follow the fence – there's a path of sorts for most of the way, about 50 yards to the left. When you come to a house ahead (A, ¾ mile) turn left to the road (50 yds) and turn right along it. Walk through Norleywood and as you leave the village turn right along the footpath opposite 'Tamarisk' (B, ⅓ mile). The path turns left to the road between two cottages (C, ½ mile). Turn right on the road. *Join **Walk 34** here.*

At the triangular junction, turn left (¼ mile, s.p. Bucklers Hard – on the map this appears to be straight on, but a wiggle in the road makes it a left turn when you come to it). Follow it round the bend at Tanners Lane (D, ¼ mile) and take a footpath on the left (E,

Norleywood

¼ mile – look back to see the signpost). Where the track turns away right (¾ mile) go straight on over the stile, bear left to another stile, then cross the field to the road (100 yds). Turn left, then take the footpath on the right (F, 30 yards, *Walk 34 rejoins here*). Keep left in the field, cross the stile, keep right in the next field, and cross the stile on the right to the road (¼ mile). Turn left.

Turn right on the track by the telephone box (G, ⅓ mile) then left at the cattle grid (200 yds) and walk between two fences until they turn away right (¼ mile). Enter the inclosure by the gate on the left and turn right on the track. When this opens out at a crossing with a broad path on the right (H, 300 yds), turn left on the narrow path in front of a stand of pines. Follow this path through Norley Wood car park, turn right on the road then left at the crossroads to return to Bull Hill car park (¾ mile). *To return to Walk 32, pass the car park and turn right on the track by the cattle grid (200 yds) to a footpath on the left (100 yds).*

Near by

The High Street of **Lymington** (2 miles) retains much of its old character; it hosts the market on Saturdays. Walk up the hill at least as far as the church before returning to the bottom of the town to visit the quay. The unusual church is of medieval origin but much altered, and derives its unique character from galleries added in the late eighteenth century. From the quay beside the busy Lymington River, the road leads in about five minutes to a small riverside park, the yacht clubs and the large marina. If you prefer to drive, there's a car park down there as well (pay-and-display).

• From Bull Hill car park turn right on the road. Turn left at the mini-roundabout (1¾ miles, s.p. Town Centre) then turn right (150 yds) and follow signs to the car park (100 yds, SZ 325957). There is pedestrian access to the High Street between the buildings at the back of the car park.

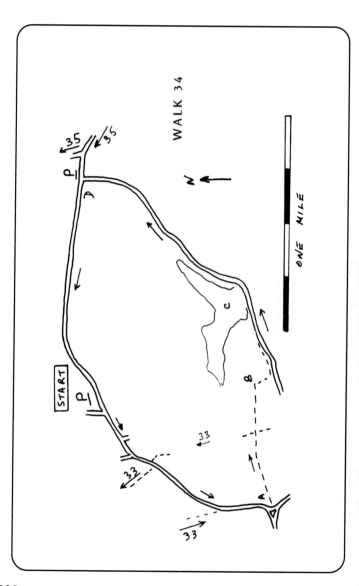

WALK 34

ONE MILE

WALK 34: EAST END TO THORNS CORNER

DISTANCE 4¼ miles (2¼ miles).

PARKING On the roadside verge in East End (SZ 368975).

From Lymington: take the B3054 (s.p. Beaulieu); go over the cattle grid (1½ miles after crossing the river) and turn right at crossroads (⅓ mile, s.p. Norleywood). Turn left at the T-junction (1½ miles, s.p. East Boldre). Park at the end of the village by the turn to Bucklers Hard (¼ mile).

From Brockenhurst: take the B3055 (s.p. Beaulieu) and turn right on the B3054 (4¾ miles, s.p. Lymington) then proceed from * below.

From Beaulieu: take the B3054 (s.p. Lymington) and turn left with it (1¼ miles, s.p. Lymington). * Take the first left (300 yds, s.p. East End), pass a turn to Bucklers Hard in East Boldre (¾ mile) and park near the next left turn (2 miles, s.p. Bucklers Hard).

Most of this walk is constrained to the road by enclosed land, and there is a short overlap with Walk 33, but nevertheless on a nice day it makes a very pleasant, quiet stroll. There are glimpses of the Solent from time to time and from one point (B) there is a view of The Needles, 9 miles to the south-west. Encouragement is provided by signposts showing that Bucklers Hard is getting ever closer. The East End Arms is passed near the start of the walk.

Sowley Pond (C) is the largest stretch of fresh water in the Forest, being over half a mile from tip to tip. It is an artificial lake — the road crosses the embankment that forms the dam across the confluence of four shallow valleys. It was first created by the monks of Beaulieu Abbey as a fishpond, and in medieval times was variously known as Colgrimesmore, Frieswater and South Leigh. Later it was to have an industrial purpose — there was an iron works at Sowley. It was set up about 1600 and used ore from Hengistbury Head and Hordle cliffs, and charcoal from the New Forest. It worked in association with a forge at

Sowley Pond

Titchfield until it acquired its own forge around 1700, giving rise to the local saying that 'there will be rain when Sowley Hammer is heard' (what its immediate neighbours said is not recorded). Its products supplied Portsmouth Dockyard and also the shipyards around Bucklers Hard on the Beaulieu River (see Walk 35). The pond provided the water supply for the wheel that drove the forge.

Directions

Follow the road through East End (s.p. Lymington), passing the Norleywood turning and The East End Arms (*Walk 33 joins here*), to a triangular junction (A, 1 mile). Turn left (on the map this appears

to be straight on, but a wiggle in the road makes it a left turn when you get there).

As you leave the bend turn left on a footpath. Keep to the left of fields, passing through a patch of woodland on the way, to a short post with a 'Solent Way' waymark (B, ½ mile). Turn right to the hedge (200 yds), turn left to the gate (300 yds), exit to the road and turn left.

Pass Sowley Pond (C) and continue to the T-junction (D, 1¼ miles). *Turn right for* **Walk 35**. Otherwise turn left (**Walk 35** *rejoins here*) to return to East End (1 mile).

To return to **Walk 33**, *go straight on through East End (s.p. Lymington), pass the right turn to Norleywood (¼ mile) then take the footpath on the right (200 yds).*

Near by

Walk 33 passed the end of **Tanners Lane** (1¾ miles), which goes down to the Solent shore. Explorations along the shore in either direction will be fairly limited, especially at high tide (a notice warns that there is no right of way above the high water mark), but you are beside the sea and the views are good – the strange-looking 'ship' to the south-west is Hurst Castle.

• From the roadside in East End, go through the village (s.p. Lymington), keeping left at the end, and take the first left (A, 1 mile, s.p. Sowley) then the first right (¼ mile, s.p. Tanners Lane). There's room for a couple of cars to park at the end of the lane (½ mile, SZ 364953) and for a few more on the shore if the tide's not too high.

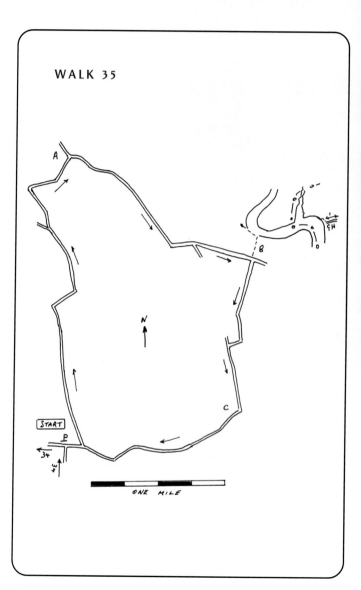

WALK 35

A

B

N

C

START

P

34

3 4

ONE MILE

WALK 35: THORNS CORNER TO BUCKLERS HARD

DISTANCE 7 miles (2½ miles).

PARKING At the roadside near Thorns Corner (SZ 386978).

From the parking place for Walk 34 in East End: take the road east (s.p. Bucklers Hard). Park opposite the first road on the right (1¼ miles, s.p. Sowley Lane).

Today you reach the end of the journey you started just a short distance away at Gilbury Hard (GH), looking across the Beaulieu River to Bucklers Hard (B). Looking the other way from the bottom of the village, Gilbury Hard is more difficult to pick out; it is half a mile downstream just as the river bends away.

Once again the route is confined to the road by enclosed land, this time of the Beaulieu Estate – you'll notice that the cottage doors are a different colour from those on the previous walk. The creators of the Solent Way also found no alternative, and the return leg follows its route. Traffic on the stretch between Beufre and Bucklers Hard (A to B) can be busy at popular times, but otherwise the roads are quiet. The limited choice of routes means that although Bucklers Hard is only 2½ miles away, the shortest alternative route to make a circular walk is 4½ miles. Assuming that walkers would find the shorter return less anticlimactic after reaching their final objective, the directions are given that way round.

'Bucklers' is thought to derive from a personal name, and a 'hard' is firm ground at the shore suitable for launching boats. Here in the eighteenth century, the 2nd Duke of Montague started the development of a seaport, Montague Town, through which he planned to import sugar from his lands in the West Indies. When these lands were ceded to the French the venture failed, and the facilities were taken in 1744 by a shipbuilder, James Wyatt. He ran into financial difficulties a few years later, and Henry Adams took

Bucklers Hard

over the yard, establishing a successful business building naval warships. Each ship required at least a thousand oaks, acquired from lands owned by the Duke of Montague (the New Forest timber was reserved by the crown for the royal dockyards). In 1793 he passed the business to two of his sons, but it failed early in the nineteenth century from a combination of more difficult circumstances and overambition.

The main street survives, said, perhaps fancifully, to be wide enough to roll a whole oak log down to the slipway. Some of the cottages have been converted into a museum, and others have been furnished as they would have been when the yard was in use. One of them is a small chapel; it was originally the cobbler's shop

for the boatyard, was used as the village school in the late nineteenth century, and became the Sunday School and chapel about a hundred years ago; it was restored in 1935. The entry fee to the various attractions is payable at the car park, but there is a public footpath through the village down to the river.

Abstemious walkers will have been ignoring the pubs regularly passed on these walks, but if you are only going to buy one drink on your circuit of the Forest, today is the day – you have an achievement to celebrate! The Master Builder's House, once the home of Henry Adams, is at the bottom of the street on the left.

On the outward leg is Beufre Farm (A), once the ox farm of Beaulieu Abbey, and near the end of the return leg is Bergerie Farm, once the sheep farm (*boeuf* and *berger* are the French for ox and shepherd respectively). At St Leonards Grange (C) are the remains of a medieval chapel and a barn, once one of the largest in England, over 200 ft long. Along the last mile or so there are glimpses across the Solent to the Isle of Wight, which at this point is about 3½ miles away.

Directions:
Walk 34 joins here. Set off eastwards along the road (s.p. Bucklers Hard) and take the first left (200 yds). Pass the left turn to East Boldre and follow the road to the junction at Beufre (A, 2½ miles). Turn right. Pass the right turn to Sowley and continue to Bucklers Hard (B, 1½ miles). Go ahead to the car park if you want to visit

207

the museum, otherwise turn left at the stile a few yards beyond the road junction and go down to the shore. You've made it; well done!

For the return leg, come back up the village and go straight ahead on the road (s.p. St Leonards). Turn left at the T-junction (¾ mile) and follow the road past St Leonards (C) back to Thorns Corner (1¾ miles). *To return to **Walk 34** go straight on.*

Near by

The village of **Beaulieu** (3½ miles) grew up beside Beaulieu Abbey. In atonement for a dispute with the Cistercians, King John granted them a large tract of land in the New Forest called *Bellus Locus Regis* – or *Beau Lieu* in Norman French – in 1204. They built what was then the largest Cistercian abbey in England, consecrated in 1246. The abbey was dissolved by Henry VIII in 1538; its materials were used for the construction of Hurst and Calshot castles, and the land sold to Thomas Wriothesley, later Earl of Southampton, an ancestor of the present owner, Lord Montague, who established the National Motor Museum here. The tidal pond between the village and the abbey was created to supply a tide mill; the present church was formerly the monks' refectory, accounting for its unusual north-south alignment. If you haven't already celebrated the completion of your journey at Bucklers Hard, you'll find The Montague Arms at the eastern end of the village.

•   From Thorns Corner go east along the road (s.p. Bucklers Hard) and take the first left (200 yds, s.p. Lodge Lane). Turn left at the T-junction near Beufre Farm (A, 2¾ miles). Turn right at the next T-junction (½ mile, the B3054) then take the first right (⅓ mile, s.p. Southampton) and first right again to the car park (100 yds, just after the garage, s.p. Village Hall, SU 386021). If full, take the next right and hope to find a space at the kerb in the High Street.

POSTSCRIPT

Today you have joined the select band of those who have walked completely around the New Forest. Welcome to the club. If you have done the walk one way, perhaps as a holiday, I hope you have enjoyed it enough to want to do it again – come back some time and follow the return legs of the walks; in the meantime, have a safe journey home. If you have been doing the circular walks, you have of course walked round the New Forest twice, once in each direction. You have 2½ miles from Bucklers Hard to return to the start of this last walk. For this I wish you a warm summer's evening, and time to dawdle along the lane and reflect on what you have encountered on your journey – the peace of the oak woodlands and the silence of the conifer plantations, the summer heather abloom, the deer who wander away patiently as you approach, the call of the woodpeckers and the curlews, the echo of startled wing beats in woodland, the ubiquitous ponies, with their foals in spring, the gentle Avon sliding along to Christchurch, the sun setting over Cranborne Chase, the cold wind on the northern plateau, the fine rich men's houses and the little cottages, the firm grass of the lawns and the squelch in the hollows, the fine days and the wet ones. A stranger visiting the New Forest for the first time might think it was all the same; we know differently, don't we?

A WEEK'S WALKING

Because each of the walks connects with the next – directions on how to make the connections are given in the text – they can be used as a basis for a single long distance walk, taking about a week. The two itineraries below are suggested as starting points for your own planning process. Both assume Beaulieu as the start and end point, and each day ends at a village. See the Introduction for a note on where to find out about accommodation.

Anticlockwise – using the outward leg of each walk

In this direction the walk follows the boundary quite closely. The total distance is 70 miles, of which nearly half is on roads, although most of them are unfenced or have verges to walk on; about 5 miles are on B-roads, the rest are on quiet, unclassified roads – but expect some traffic on summer weekends; A-roads are not used, although 2 miles of the first day are close to the A326.

Heather in bloom,
Blackwell Common

1. Beaulieu to Ashurst (Walks 2 to 7) – 11 miles

Miss out Walk 1; take the B3054 east from Beaulieu, turn right at the junction by The Royal Oak (1 mile, s.p. Holbury – don't turn right again to Exbury), pass The Bridge Tavern (1¼ miles) then take the first left (¼ mile, Park Lane) to join Walk 2 at B on the sketch map.

2. Ashurst to Nomansland (Walks 8 to 12) – 11 miles

(a) Miss out Walk 11 – stay on the road from Crock Hill (B on Walk 10) to the crossroads at Furzley (¾ mile) then turn right on to Walk 12.

(b) After Walk 12, continue to Nomansland on Walk 13 (A, ¾ mile).

3. Nomansland to Godshill (Walks 13 to 18) – 9 miles

4. Godshill to Burley (Walks 19 to 23) – 11 miles

From Smugglers' Road car park (D) at the end of Walk 23, turn left on the road, keep right at the junction, and follow it through Burley Street to Burley (2 miles).

5. Burley to Brockenhurst (Walks 25 to 29) – 14 miles

(a) From Burley, miss out Walk 24 by taking the road south from the War Memorial (s.p. Bransgore) to Burbush Hill car park (1 mile) at the start of Walk 25.

(b) Also miss out the westward loop at the start of Walk 25 (via A and B); just go straight down the road to the crossroads (C, 1 mile) and turn left.

6. Brockenhurst to Beaulieu (Walks 30 to 35) – 14 miles

(a) Use the return leg of Walk 35 as follows: ignore the left turn near the start of the walk and take the first road on the right (1¾ miles) to Buckler's Hard (C, ¾ mile).

(b) For Beaulieu (2 miles), go down to the river at Buckler's Hard and turn left on the footpath. Turn right by the boatyard on to the Riverside Walk and right again when it returns to the footpath.

Clockwise – using the return leg of each walk

This walk is mostly inside the boundary, across open heathland or through woodland. The need for the individual circular walks to return to a car park brings the route back to the boundary frequently; this makes it wiggle around a bit, but the purpose is to enjoy the walking, not to get from A to B as expeditiously as possible. The total distance is around 80 miles, about a quarter being on roads.

1. Beaulieu to Brockenhurst (Walks 35 to 30) – 15 miles

(a) From Beaulieu take the footpath on the left of The Montague Arms to Bucklers Hard (2 miles). Go up through the village to join Walk 35 at B on the sketch map.

(b) Miss out Walk 30; stay with Walk 31 to the river and follow it upstream to the road junction (½ mile). Turn left to Brockenhurst (1 mile, B to A on Walk 30).

2. Brockenhurst to Burley (Walks 29 to 24) – 14 miles

(a) From Brockenhurst, go over the level crossing and take the second left (100 yds, Church Lane) to join the return leg of Walk 29 heading for the church (E).

(b) Burley is at D on Walk 24.

3. Burley to Godshill
(Walks 23 to 19) – 15 miles
(a) Start from Burley by joining the return leg of Walk 24 at D.
(b) At the end of Walk 19, get to Godshill by using the directions for returning to Walk 18.

4. Godshill to Bramshaw
(Walks 18 to 13) – 13 miles
(a) From Godshill, join Walk 18 at D by taking the bridleway opposite the Village Hall.
(b) For the purpose of this walk, assume the centre of Bramshaw to be at the school, between C and D on Walk 13.

5. Bramshaw to Ashurst
(Walks 13 to 8) – 10 miles
(a) Start from Bramshaw by going north on the B3079 (C to D on Walk 13).
(b) Miss out Walk 11; at the end of Walk 12 turn right at the crossroads to join Walk 10 near C.

6. Ashurst to Beaulieu
(Walks 7 to 2) – 13 miles
(a) Join Walk 7 in Ashurst at the car park by the hospital gate.
(b) Miss out Walk 1; return to Beaulieu (2½ miles) by turning right on the road at F on Walk 2.

Following pages: Latchmore Bottom from Abbots Well.

SELECTED BIBLIOGRAPHY

1. Books

The New Forest, Colin R. Tubbs (New Forest Ninth Century Trust, 2002)

The New Forest, John R Wise (S. R. Publishers Ltd, 1971 [1862])

A Wild Heritage, Terry Heathcote (Ensign Publications, 1990)

Discovering the New Forest, Terry Heathcote (Halsgrove, 1997)

Explore the New Forest, ed. Don Small (The Forestry Commission/HMSO, 1975)

Ordnance Survey Leisure Guide: The New Forest, ed. Donna Wood (AA/Ordnance Survey, 1987)

The New Forest, Philip Allison and Maldwin Drummond (Pioneer Publications, 1979)

New Forest Documents, ed. D J Stagg (Hampshire County Council, 1979)

The New Forest, Heywood Sumner (The Dolphin Press, 1972 [1924])

Cuckoo Hill: The Book of Gorley, Heywood Sumner (Bellew Publishing, 1987 [1910])

Heywood Sumner's Wessex, ed. Barry Cunliffe (Ray Gasson & Associates, 1985)

The New Forest: 900 Years After, Peter Tate (Macdonald and Jane's Publishers Ltd, 1979)

Pollards, People, and Ponies, Mike Walford (Short Publications, 1979)

Portrait of the New Forest, Brian Vesey-Fitzgerald (Robert Hale Ltd, 1966)

Forest Reflections, ed. H. Pasmore and M. Heinst (Forest Views, 1995)

Ashurst: A New Forest Railway Village, Peter Roberts (Nova Foresta Publishing, 1998)

Buckler's Hard: A Rural Shipbuilding Centre, A. J, Holland (Kenneth Mason, 1985)

Records of Burley: Aspects of a New Forest Village, F. Hardcastle (Chameleon International, 1987 [1950])

Castleman's Corkscrew: The Southampton and Dorchester Railway 1844–1848, J. G. Cox (City of Southampton, 1975)
The Lymington Branch, P.Paye (The Oakwood Press, 1979)

Smuggling in Hampshire and Dorset 1700–1850, Geoffrey Morley (Countryside Books, 1983)
The Royal Forests of England, Raymond Grant (Allan Sutton Publishing Ltd, 1991)
Forests of Britain, Thomas Hinde (Victor Gollancz Ltd, 1985)
Dawn, Dusk, and Deer, Arthur Cadman (The Sportsman's Press, 1989 [1966])
The Old Telegraphs, Geoffrey Wilson (Phillimore, 1976)
Place Names of Hampshire, Richard Coates (Batsford, 1989)
Victoria County History (University of London, 1900–1912)
The Buildings of England: Hampshire and the Isle of Wight, Nikolaus Pevsner and David Lloyd (Penguin Books, 1967)

2. Websites

National Park Authority	www.newforestnpa.gov.uk
New Forest District Council	www.newforest.gov.uk
Forestry Commission	www.forestry.gov.uk/newforest
Hampshire County Council	www.hants.gov.uk/newforest
The New Forest Association	www.newforestassociation.com
Verderers of the New Forest	www.verderers.org.uk
Commoners Defence Association	www.newforestcommoners.co.uk
Hampshire Wildlife Trust	www.hwt.org.uk
New Forest Equine Directory	www.nfed.co.uk
New Forest Pony Breeding and Cattle Society	www.newforestpony.com

SELECTED BIBLIOGRAPHY

Natural England   www.naturalengland.org.uk
Council for National Parks   www.cnp.org.uk/new_forest.htm
Southampton University   www.geodata.soton.ac.uk/
                                    newforest/public/index.html
BBC Southampton   www.bbc.co.uk/southampton/
                                    features/newforest/index.shtml
Countryside Agency   www.countryside.gov.uk
English Nature   www.english-nature.org.uk

Visitor information, accomodation, travel etc.
New Forest District Council   www.thenewforest.co.uk
Forestry Commission   www.forestholidays.co.uk
Other useful sites can be found on the internet by searching for
New Forest Accommodation

Traveline   www.traveline.org.uk
National Rail Enquiries   www.nationalrail.co.uk
Hampshire County Council   www3.hants.gov.uk/
                                    passengertransport
Wilts & Dorset Bus Co   www.wdbus.co.uk
Solent Blue Line   www.solentblueline.com
South West Trains   www.swtrains.co.uk
Virgin Trains   www.virgintrains.co.uk
Hythe Ferry   www.hytheferry.co.uk

INDEX

Page numbers in **bold** type refer to photographs

INDEX

INDEX

INDEX